With best wishes

Per Regards
Rochelle Schatz

pain & *pleasure*

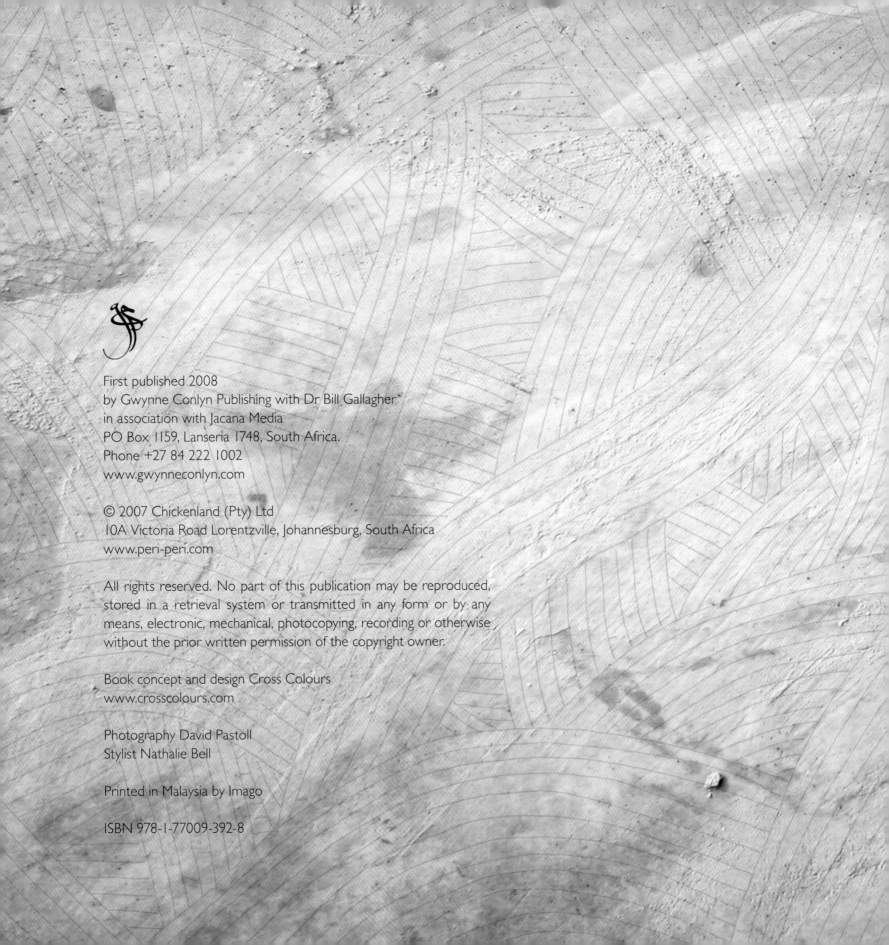

First published 2008
by Gwynne Conlyn Publishing with Dr Bill Gallagher*
in association with Jacana Media
PO Box 1159, Lanseria 1748, South Africa.
Phone +27 84 222 1002
www.gwynneconlyn.com

Book concept and design Cross Colours
www.crosscolours.com

Photography David Pastoll
Stylist Nathalie Bell

Printed in Malaysia by Imago

ISBN 978-1-77009-392-8

peri-peri the contrasts & contradictions of the african bird's eye chilli

Photography David Pastoll
Illustrations Mike Saal and Elzanne de Klerk
Art direction, design and text Cross Colours

The African Bird's Eye Chilli is rich in contradiction: from its magical role in ancient African tribal healing to its undeniable presence among emerging 21st Century food trends. It makes for heated conversation...

With this book we wanted to convert some of the myths surrounding this little scarlet pod to fact, by researching and providing the science behind the many (mis)perceptions and beliefs. At times it was really challenging to lay some of these myths to rest and adopt newly discovered science as fact. Thank you to everyone that so passionately participated in these heated discussions – your contributions shaped the content – and you hold the treasured results in your hands.

To Peri-Peri lovers all around the world – you are the reason for this book (let us celebrate our addiction).

It's been over 10 years since our first desire to create a credible reference work about Peri-Peri. Since then the scope of the project changed a couple of times as we all got older & wiser, as more research on the topic became available and as new people passionately joined where others could no longer support. Many incredible people gave unselfishly of their time, skill, knowledge and talent to make this book happen. We've tried to keep record of everyone, and full credit is given in the acknowledgements. A very sincere THANK YOU to everyone that has lived, loved, laughed, cried and celebrated with us on this journey.

Rochelle Schaetzl
Johannesburg, 2008

contents

As I look back over the last three decades and review the impact of Peri-Peri, it is remarkable how it has grown into a 'must have' ingredient for every chef.

foreword - the magic of Peri-Peri

Chillies not only warm the soul but add excitement to so many recipes and cooking styles. Packed with flavour, its following continues to grow globally.

I have been fortunate in my role as Honorary Life President of the World Association of Chefs Societies to have travelled and tasted many countries' cuisines, and it is very hard to think of where chilli does not fit onto a menu.

The name Peri-Peri is becoming synonymous with an exciting flavour explosion in the mouth. Fresh or dried, in soups or stews, pastas or desserts, it has gained the moral high ground.

Today, some of the world's greatest chefs have realised the full potential of this chilli and have made signature recipes that have gone on to become classics.

The African continent has a rich heritage built around the mystique of herbs, spices and a melting pot of influences from its many and varied cultures and people.

The world over food has become more internationalised with instant communications, shorter travelling time – the East meets West, South meets North global village has certainly become a reality. This has led to chefs being more ambitious and more resourceful and our customers willing to take a leap of faith in trying and tasting new flavours.

Once you have enjoyed that remarkable taste of Peri-Peri, you are invariably hooked. Some even graduate to go on and become real chilli heads.

But it is a recognised fact that this ingredient has more impact than any other herb or spice you can think of.

This book gives the reader a wonderful insight into the characteristics of Peri-Peri, its tremendous medicinal value, as well as the culinary inside story.

It is packed with wonderful stories and anecdotes that will enthuse the reader.

We congratulate the authors and the many outstanding chefs who have contributed very exciting dishes that make this a unique collector's item for every lover of good food.

Dr Bill Gallagher

Honorary Life President, World Association of Chefs Societies
Honorary President, South African Chefs Association

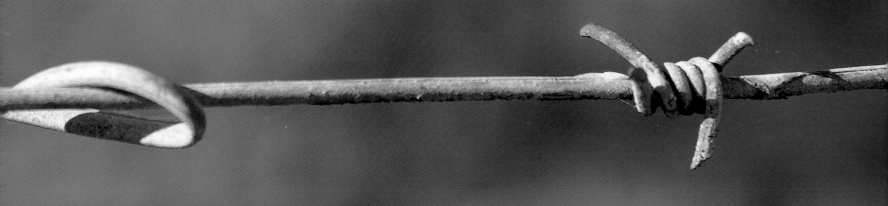

This is a book about something so popular and so common, and yet something that most people know almost nothing about. While it is never taken for granted, who really knows its story?

introduction

The chilli has been exciting our taste buds and bringing joy to the lives of human beings for millennia. It has been used variously in our cooking for its medicinal and health-giving properties and even, eye-wateringly, in our sex lives. It is estimated that chillies form part of the daily diet of almost a quarter of the world's population.

Paradoxically, it is precisely because its use is so widespread that the story of how it came to be, is elusive. As you will see, while the chilli is American in origin, the variants that have been imported to other places adapt quickly, becoming new plants in their own right. More than that, these new chillies always become a source of pride among the citizens of their adopted homes.

The African Bird's Eye Chilli is an especially pungent little chilli that evokes a level of passion that is inversely proportional to its size. Possibly the world's smallest chilli, it generates the world's warmest reaction. The African Bird's Eye Chilli is grown all over south-east Africa and looks and tastes like no other chilli in the world. It is uniquely African and has been embraced with real love. Just as your family wouldn't be what it is without you, so Africa wouldn't be the place it is without the African Bird's Eye Chilli. The plant has adapted to the African soil. And in turn, our recipes have evolved to suit it, from the berebere of Ethiopia to the molho de piri-piri of Mozambique.

Not everybody calls it the African Bird's Eye Chilli. It's also known as Piri-Piri, Pili-Pili or Peli-Peli – regional variants of a Lingala and Swahili (both languages are Sub-Saharan African in origin) term meaning 'very hot'. It is possible that 'very' is a polite substitute for a slightly more expressive word, but you get the idea.

Nowadays, Peri-Peri is widely accepted as the preferred name. But no one is going to insist on it. Because once you've discovered Peri-Peri, how you say it simply doesn't matter. What is important is what it can do for you.

People who enjoy Peri-Peri have found it to be addictive. This isn't based on any kind of scary physical or psychological dependence. It is addictive for the simple reason that it is delicious and because it makes almost anything else delicious when added to it – in other words, it has a generous spirit. And because those who love the chilli become inured to its heat, they are forced to eat it in greater and greater quantities to rediscover their first experience of it.

Equally addictive are the stories of the chilli and Peri-Peri itself. The contrasts and contradictions of Peri-Peri are what make it so interesting. What we know about it doesn't always add up, and there are wildly differing accounts of its history. The contradictions pile up like reams of typescript until an ungainly and conflicting manuscript emerges.

Peri-Peri can be introduced to almost any recipe – savoury or sweet. It brings pleasure not only to the eating of a meal, but to its preparation as well. However, that pleasure has a distinct edge to it – there is a fine balance between the pleasure of 'just enough' and the pain of 'too much'.

So Peri-Peri is a spice that brings pleasure and pain. The 'ands' in this book are at once contradictory and consistent. Or, to put it another way, there is consistency in the nature of Peri-Peri's contradictions. The 'ands' work together or, alternatively, set one thought off against another. An 'and' can bring two distinct ideas together or it can keep them apart.

A good story that is remembered and talked about never quite adds up. The loose ends are what keep us intrigued. We continue to ponder the inconsistencies, the little lapses in internal logic. Trying to shoehorn everything into a single book is almost as difficult as trying to make sense of Peri-Peri's origins.

Those who eat Peri-Peri regularly attest to the delight it brings to otherwise ordinary meals and to the generally uplifting effect it has on their everyday lives. Let it be said that there is just as much pleasure to be had in the story of this little chilli.

heart & heat

Where does the heart of Peri-Peri lie? The clue is right there in its alias, the African Bird's Eye Chilli. Right in the heart of south-east Africa is a cluster of countries where Peri-Peri grows wild, and is cultivated: Malawi, Mozambique, Zimbabwe and South Africa. The climate of these countries is warm enough to provide just the right amount of stress to make Peri-Peri the fiery ingredient it is.

storytelling

It is almost impossible to untangle the many myths that surround the discovery of Peri-Peri. This is unfortunate because discovery is perhaps the single most important theme in the story of Peri-Peri. Every day, someone somewhere in the world is discovering Peri-Peri for the first time.

Those who already love and use Peri-Peri feel a twinge of jealousy when they imagine how wonderful it would be to again be a Peri-Peri virgin and feel for the first time the rush as it enters your system. Experiencing Peri-Peri for the first time, chasing that thrill, is what all Peri-Peri lovers are doing all the time.

But then again, every experience of Peri-Peri is a rediscovery of flavour, passion, delight, and it is almost always as thrilling as your first time.

the heat of the kitchen

For people who love to cook, the kitchen is a place of passion, excitement and experimentation. Some people like to have music on while they cook. Others prefer silence so that they can concentrate on the sounds of bubbling stock, the crackle of roasting meat, the sharp snapping of a knife chopping vegetables, the clanging of pots and the rattle of cutlery.

In Laura Esquivel's novel *Like Water for Chocolate*, the main character, Tita, is a wonder in the kitchen. It so happens that when she is cooking, the emotions she experiences seep magically into the meal. This means that when her family and friends eat the food she prepares, they experience pangs of great sadness or outbursts of overwhelming laughter.

It cannot be argued that a meal is about more than the sum total of its ingredients: you add this and that, mix them together, turn up the heat and – if you're really working at it and doing it with pleasure – miracles occur. The combination of flavours, colours and textures conspire to create something truly special. Peri-Peri is the ingredient that brings this magic to life. It enhances the tastes of other flavours. It inspires and spurs people on to greater things. It's a not-so-little thing called passion. It isn't just another spice, it's a catalyst.

I have the chilli

23

So the spiritual and physical home of Peri-Peri is south-east Africa. But not quite. The chilli is in fact originally from South America. (In parts of Brazil, for example, the malagueta chilli, which is very similar to Peri-Peri, is grown.)

citizenship

People have been eating chillies since about 7 500BC. During the course of several archaeological digs in Tehuacan in Mexico, dried chilli seeds and fruit have been discovered in burial grounds 9 000 years old. This means that chillies are one of the oldest cultivated crops of the Americas.

The chilli has, over the course of the last five hundred years, travelled across the globe. It has made a home for itself on almost every continent. But even when the chilli settles in a new country, it doesn't stay in one place. In Africa, Peri-Peri chillies journey up and down the continent as we cultivate and transport them for use in our daily lives.

No other spice has spread so quickly. Columbus brought the chilli back from the New World in 1493. It spread quickly through Europe, arriving in Italy by 1535 and in Germany by 1542. Portuguese explorers, after discovering the Cape of Good Hope in 1487, introduced it to Africa and then to India in 1498. Within a few decades, European travellers in Asia found that it was used in cooking there and were mystified as to its origin. As a result, chilli is known by many different names: pepper, chili, chile, chilli, aji, paprika.

There are several reasons for the chilli being the international treasure it is. The seeds are easily transportable. They can be germinated in favourable conditions after several years of storage. Then, when planted, they acclimatise quickly, adapting to almost every country in which they find themselves.

The origins of Peri-Peri are, like the African continent, full of contradictions. *Capsicum* is the genus of plant to which the chilli belongs, and the family seems to be American in origin. If this is the case, how can Peri-Peri be truly African? This question can be answered by referring to something the French call *terroir*. Literally, it means 'soil', but as a term it's virtually impossible to translate since it means so much more.

Terroir is a term that describes the combination of soil, climate and the geographical location that makes coffee or wine grown in a certain region distinctly different from that grown elsewhere. It includes all aspects of an environment, such as the altitude, the degree of a slope affecting the sunlight's intensity, its aspect, whether it is north or south facing, the prevailing winds and even the water table.

the tropics

Most *Capsicum* species are vulnerable to environmental conditions and will hybridise extremely quickly to combat environmental conditions. Remarkably, some chilli seeds harvested in Mexico and planted in Africa will produce chillies completely different from those of their parent plants. And then, if offspring from the new plant are reintroduced to the original Mexican soil, they will produce yet another slightly different chilli.

So chillies introduced to Africa very quickly became Peri-Peri. Environmental conditions resulted in chillies with a different flavour and heat. In other words, only the *terroir* of south-east Africa can produce Peri-Peri. It is native to this part of the world and no other chilli in the world is quite like it.

Peri-Peri is a native of the tropics, the humid, languid parts of the world. Its heart lies in a colourful place where conversation happens at loud volume and where you are made to feel welcome; a place where people eat hot food so that they perspire, in the hope that a breeze will catch them and cool their skin just as efficiently as a dip in the ocean would.

Sir Laurens van der Post said, "the person who has once acquired a taste in the tropics for African chillies becomes an addict".

The same could be said of Africa. The people who visit, often become addicted to it and end up staying. There is something about Africa that draws people to it. Once you've experienced its warmth and vitality, it's extremely hard to imagine being anywhere else.

The continent of Africa is so alluring because of its people, their naturally welcoming nature, and their sense of kinship. This even has a name – *Ubuntu*. The concept of *Ubuntu* is a purely African, taken from the Zulu phrase, *umuntu ngumuntu ngabantu*. Loosely translated, this means, "You are who you are because of other people". It is a feeling of companionship and a common bond, a sense of awareness that we are who we are through our connections with others – and maybe even defined that way.

It can be said that Peri-Peri does a similar thing by bringing people together. It is one of those rare ingredients that brings families and friends together in a chorus of laughter, talking and eating. It certainly doesn't encourage quiet introspection. Its heat brings people out of themselves and encourages warmth. It fosters friendship. It is fitting that Peri-Peri should come from a continent with a population that has this ideology, which is based on finding your identity through your interaction with others. South-east Africa truly is the spiritual home of Peri-Peri, as well as its physical home.

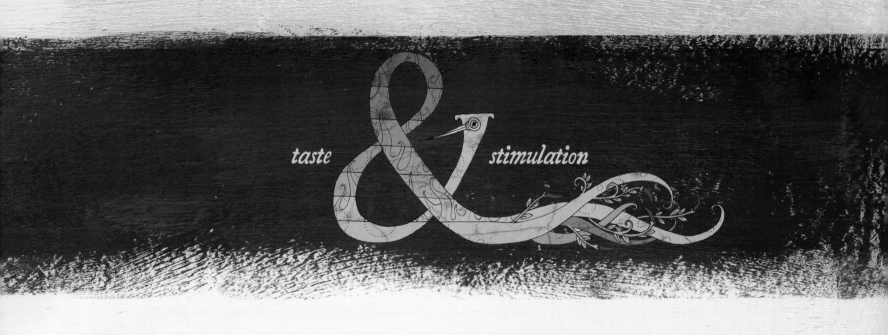

taste & stimulation

Peri-Peri is about more than mere taste. That is only the beginning – Peri-Peri awakens your taste buds and sends a rush of physical pleasure down through your chest to your stomach. Its heat is invigorating, and it arouses a sense of excitement in a way that no other ingredient can. But what makes it so hot and so exhilarating?

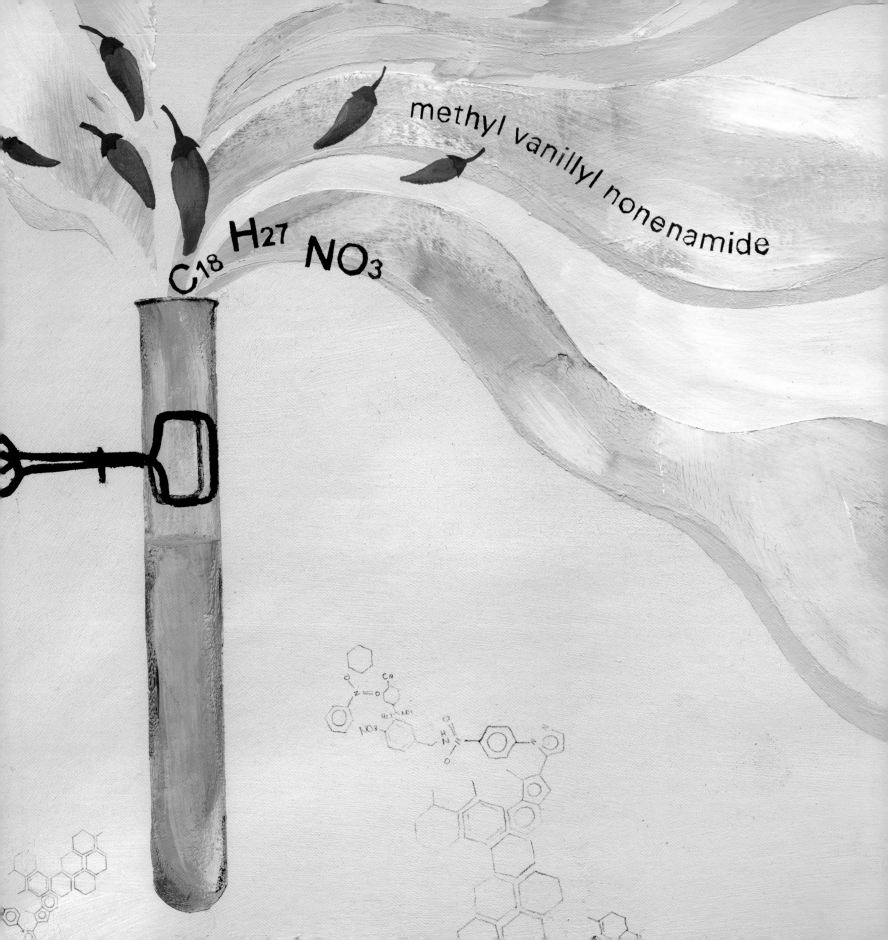

methyl vanillyl nonenamide

$C_{18} H_{27} NO_3$

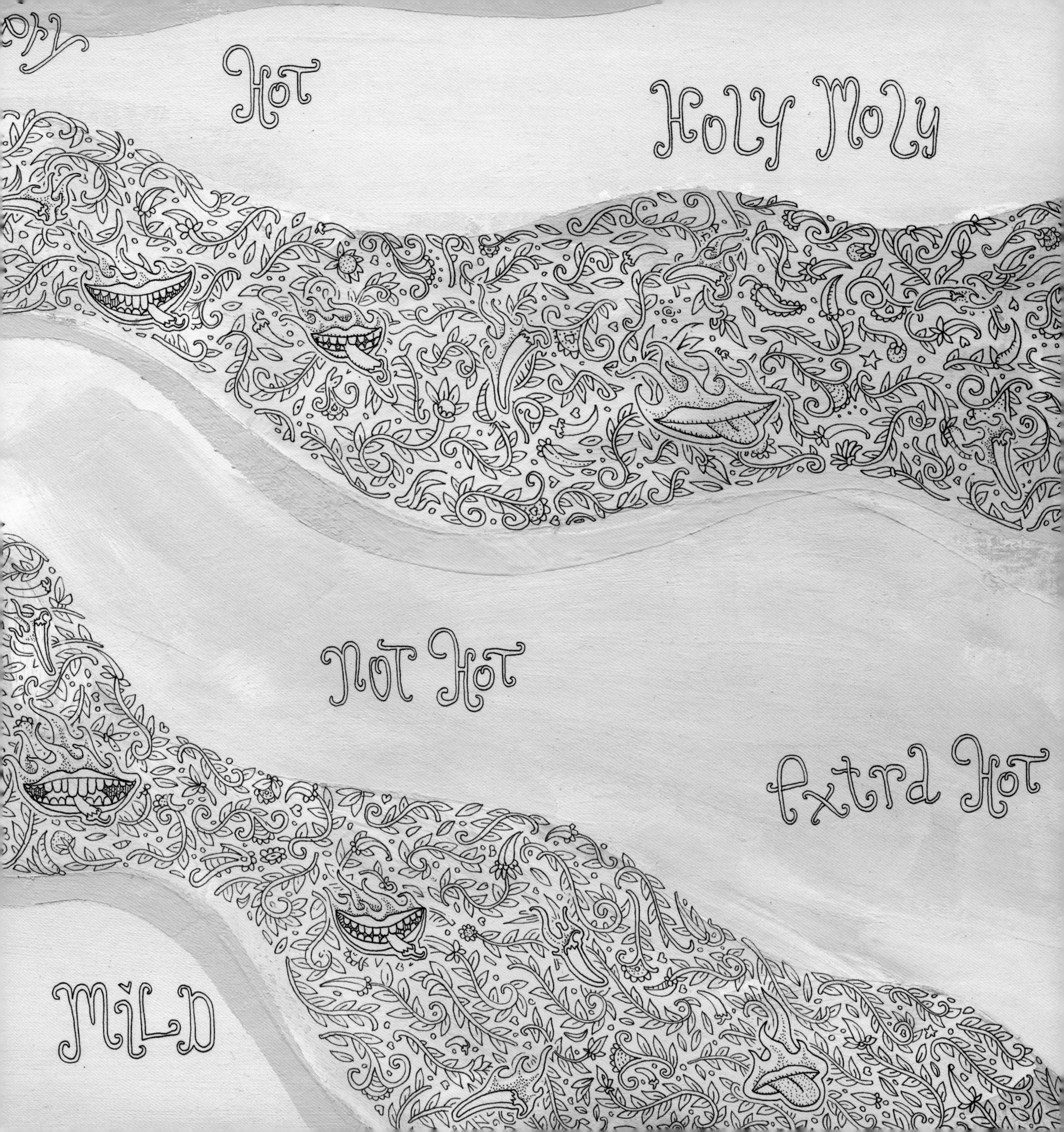

Hot

Holy Moly

Not Hot

Extra Hot

Mild

The heat, or rather pungency of Peri-Peri depends on the amount of Capsaicin it contains. Capsaicin is the powerful chemical compound (also known as methyl vanillyl nonenamide) that gives chillies their vitality and gets the heart racing when we eat them. It is the main Capsaicinoid in a chilli, one of five others that are collectively the active constituent of all chillies. Capsaicin and Dihydrocapsaicin are more or less twice as pungent as the other Capsaicinoids in a chilli – Nordihydrocapsaicin, Homodihydrocapsaicin and HomoCapsaicin.

stimulation

Capsaicin on its own is virtually colourless. Produced by glands along the points where the placenta and the internal wall of the chilli meet, Capsaicin is one of the most pungent compounds known to scientists. The seeds of a chilli are not hot in themselves, but they absorb Capsaicin because they are so close to the placenta – and this is why many people believe it is the seeds that contain heat.

The smaller the chilli, the hotter it is likely to be. Smaller chillies contain proportionally more seeds and veins than larger varieties. The seeds make up about 50% of a dried chilli's weight. And those seeds contain up to 80% of a chilli's strength.

The Capsaicin content of Peri-Peri can range from about 0.1% in mild chillies, to 1.3% in the ones that are more pungent.

200,000 - 300,000

100,000 - 350,000

60,000 - 80,000

30,000 - 50,000

2,500 - 5,000

500 - 1,000

0 - 100

Experience teaches Peri-Peri lovers that if ever we find our mouths on fire, the most effective antidotes are dairy products, like yoghurt or milk. Contrary to popular opinion, a drink of cold water won't help much. It will actually feel as though the heat is increasing. When Peri-Peri touches your tongue, it stimulates the open nerve endings between your taste buds. This 'irritating' sensation is what we perceive as heat. Capsaicin is not water soluble because it is oil based. It can only be dissolved by an oil-based solvent, and therefore only the fat molecules in dairy products will actually wash it away.

experience

If you are eating a meal with lots of Peri-Peri, you will, after a while, feel as though your tongue has been overpowered. It lies back in your mouth limply, as if in a state of post-coital bliss. So it simply isn't a good time to uncork that expensive bottle of Chablis. Try something a little less extravagant. A fairly sweet late harvest wine will do fine.

In the same way that the flavour of beer complements an Indian curry, so too it does for Peri-Peri. You need a full beer with a slightly flowery (meaning fruity) aroma. A cider will do just as nicely. However, it should be noted that the gas bubbles in beer or cider do increase the 'irritation' on your tongue, and this might make the Peri-Peri seem even hotter. As non-alcoholic alternatives, sparkling grape and apple juices are as good.

Chillies and their Scoville Heat Units

0 - 100 most sweet pepper varieties

500 - 1 000 most new mexican peppers

2 500 - 5 000 jalapeno peppers

30 000 - 50 000 cayenne peppers

60 000 - 80 000 Peri-Peri

100 000 - 350 000 thai peppers

200 000 - 300 000 most habanero peppers

Peri-Peri is a crop that is widely in demand. Its considerable strength means that the flavour and heat you can extract from it is far greater than what you can extract from larger, weaker varieties of chilli. Spice manufacturers compete with Oleoresin manufacturers in attempting to buy Peri-Peri. Oleoresin is an extract of chillies with a concentrated pungency and a rich colour, used as an ingredient in foods, medicines and cosmetics.

It is often difficult for the manufacturers that process and distribute spices, seasonings, marinades and sauces to procure Peri-Peri. Africa is an unstable continent, not only politically and socially, but meteorologically too.

home & away

In the countries where Peri-Peri is farmed, the subsistence farmers grow it to earn an income over and above the crops they grow for their own use. Chillies are usually sold to manufacturers in dried form. However, during the drying process, Peri-Peri loses most of its weight. So to produce a certain number of kilograms of dried chillies, a far greater amount of fresh chillies has to be harvested. Harvesting is time consuming and painstakingly happens by hand. They might produce an excess of chillies, which will be bought up by agents. Agents liaise with many farmers and purchase more than just Peri-Peri. They might also be in the market for cayenne pepper, coriander, turmeric or goodness knows what else.

The agent will supply manufacturers with the amount of Peri-Peri they require for the coming period. Manufacturers tend to 'buy forward', which means anticipating what they will need and purchasing in advance. A sample will be sent ahead so that an ASTA (American Spice Trade Association) analytical test can be run. This involves checking the colour, flavour and heat level of the sample to ascertain the overall quality of the consignment. If the sample is satisfactory, the consignment will be dispatched.

On the lush hilltops and mountains of Malawi, Mozambique and Zimbabwe, Peri-Peri chillies are dried under the African sun, packed into hessian sacks and loaded onto trucks. When the Peri-Peri is headed for export, the trucks will carry their loads to the nearest harbour. The Peri-Peri is then put onto container ships and transported to spice manufacturers.

When there is a delivery of Peri-Peri at a spice manufacturer, the Capsaicin content of the chillies causes a chorus of coughing and sneezing among the employees. At first, the chillies are sorted by hand. The contents of a hessian sack are dumped onto a sorting table and it is the job of several people to pick through the tiny, crisp chillies. The sorters wear white latex gloves that very quickly become oily and tinged with a saffron colour. Among the expected twigs and birds' feathers, the sorters have, over the years, found bicycle parts, wool, screws, lengths of wire, and even jewellery and other trinkets.

The hand-sorted Peri-Peri is then put through a steam sterilisation process to kill any potential aflatoxins (toxic compounds produced by mould) and other bacteria. During the milling process, the Peri-Peri is ground to either a fine or a coarse powder, depending on its intended use. Peri-Peri might then be packaged on its own, or taken through a blending process with other spices for use in sauces or meat products. Finally, the chillies are split into batch packs. These vary in size, according to what the manufacturer's clients require.

In 1912, an American scientist, Wilbur Scoville developed an original method for testing piquancy. He called it the Scoville Organoleptic Test and as he devised it, a solution of the chilli pepper extract was diluted in sugar water until the heat was no longer detectable to the tongue. This degree of dilution gave its measure on the Scoville scale, in Scoville Heat Units, or SHU.

To illustrate this, take pure Capsaicin as an example. It has a Scoville rating of over 15 000 000. This means that you would have to add 15 000 litres of water to neutralise the burning sensation of one gram of pure Capsaicin.

science

A chilli plant grown in northern India, the bhut jolokia ('ghost chilli') allegedly measures 855 000 SHU, and a particular sample over 1 000 000 SHU. Peri-Peri, on the other hand, has a maximum rating of about 80 000 SHU. It isn't, however, a strictly accurate gauge of a chilli's pungency, because of its reliance on human tasters. What's hot for one person isn't necessarily hot for another. It does, however, work as a general means of comparison.

Pungency of Capsicums and Their Oleoresins

Method 21.0

(Scoville Heat Test)

Purpose: To determine pungency in capsicum spices and oleoresins.

A. Apparatus:
1. Erlenmeyer flask, narrow neck, 125 ml. w
2. Pipette, serological, 1 ml. capacity, 0.01
3. Pipettes, volumetric transfer 2 ml. and
4. Volumetric flasks, stoppered, 50 ml.
5. Funnel, analytical 58°, short stem
6. Filter paper, Whatman No. 1, 12
7. Paper cups.

B. Reagents:
1. Ethyl alcohol, 95%

$$\text{... area peak 3}$$

$$\frac{\text{...saicin area of sample} \times \text{ppm ...}}{\text{...in area of standard} \times \text{...}}$$

$$\frac{\text{...in} \times 15}{000,000 \text{ Scoville})}$$

capsaicin to Scoville

Scoville, units

150

1,500

the scoville heat test

A small measure of flaked Peri-Peri is placed in a flask, covered in ethanol and left to stand for 16 hours. The ethanol extracts the Capsaicin and a little colour from the chillies.

To feel the heat of a 70 000 SHU Peri-Peri chilli, 0,31ml of extract is diluted in 0,63ml of the sugar-water solution. The mixture is then tasted. If a burn is felt at the back of the throat, then the chillies being tested will be allocated that rating. Usually, the test will take place on a lower measurement and the tester will work his or her way up until the burn is felt and the measurement is set there.

Because the 'burn' of a chilli is so subjective, a panel of four or five people will perform the taste test. While the Scoville test isn't the definitive measurement tool, it does offer a way of gauging a chilli's strength. This is necessary to guarantee some degree of consistency in the heat of products that are prepared using Peri-Peri. (There's no good in someone deciding that they like a mild sauce, if the sauce in the next bottle labelled identically makes them feel like a small bomb has detonated on their tongue.) After establishing the heat level of a load of chillies, manufacturers can blend them with either hotter or milder chillies to regulate the heat.

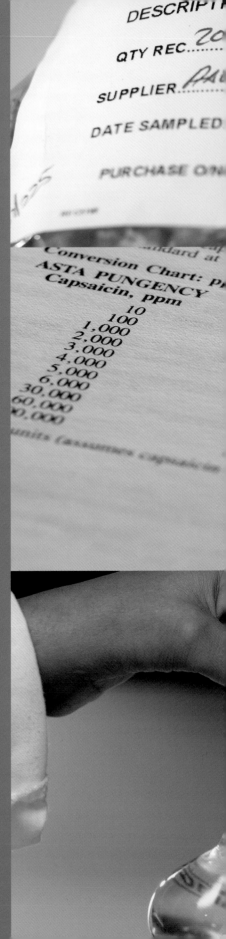

BIRDS EYE CHILLIES

DATE REC

BATCH No

n × 15
0,000 Scoville)

apsaicin to Scoville

Scoville, units
150
1,500
15,000
30,000 –
45,000 –
60,000 –
75,000
90,000

Sample

hplc

If we wanted to be boring and fogeyish, we could say that it is the way of many modern things that they lack romance. A process known as HPLC (high-performance liquid chromatography or high-pressure liquid chromatography) analyses a chilli's Capsaicin content, its flavour, colour and its overall quality. All that's required is for a lab technician to squirt a few millilitres of chilli extract into a slot in a computer. What this process lacks in nostalgic, hands-on methodology, it makes up for in its startling scientific accuracy. The process isolates the elements of the substance being analysed or, in other words, obtains pure chemical compounds from a mixture of compounds. In very simple terms, the process can be compared to warming a glass of cognac or brandy in your hands which then releases the odours and flavours captured in the liquid.

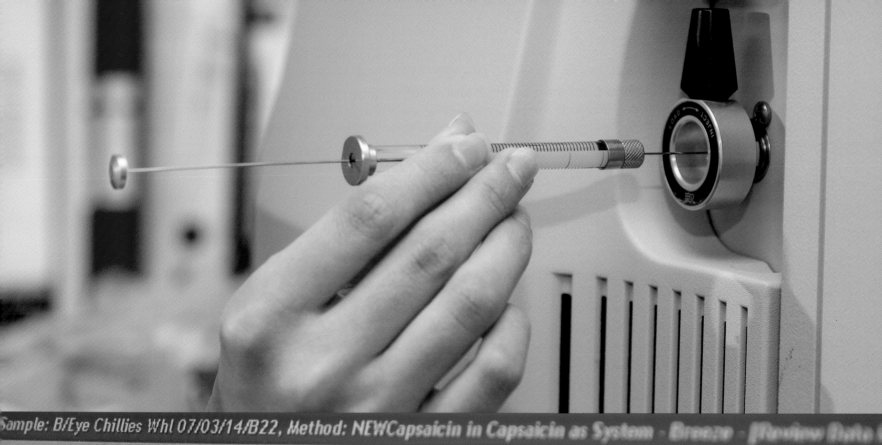

Sample: B/Eye Chillies Whl 07/03/14/B22, Method: NEWCapsaicin in Capsaicin as System - Breeze - [Review Data ...

Edit   View   Plot   Process   Navigate   Options   Window   Messages   Help

View
Method

Find
Data

- Injections:
  - STD 1 5uL - Vial: 1
    - Injection: 1
  - STD 2 10uL - Vial: 2
    - Injection: 1
  - STD 3 20uL - Vial: 3
    - Injection: 1
  - Blank - Vial: 4
    - Injection: 1
  - Blank - Vial: 5
    - Injection: 1
  - Blank - Vial: 6
    - Injection: 1
  - B/Eye Chillies Whl 07/03/14/B22 - Vi...
    - Injection: 1
  - B/Eye Chillies Whl 07/03/14/B22 - Vi...
  - B/Eye Chillies Whl 07/03/14/B22 - Vi...
  - B/Eye Chillies Whl 07/03/14/B22 - Vi...
  - B/Eye Chillies Whl 07/03/14/B22 - Vi...

roots & routes

The story of Peri-Peri involves countless journeys, over many hundreds of thousands of kilometres.

The roots of the individual plants may not penetrate the earth very far at all,

but the degree to which Peri-Peri is entrenched in our everyday lives is a result of the depth of its history.

Chillies and humankind — we go way back.

explorers

Christopher Columbus had been attempting to find a route to the East for the Spanish by travelling west to avoid Africa, which was under the control of the Portuguese. In doing so, not only did he discover North America, but he also became the first European to discover chilli. Some are of the opinion that this was his greater achievement.

When, under the impression that he had reached India, Columbus tasted chilli, he thought it must be a red variety of pepper. He wrote in his journal, "there is plenty of aji, which is their pepper... and all the people eat nothing else, it being very wholesome".

Black pepper, because it was imported from Asia, was very expensive. The chilli, being easier to grow, was a cheaper alternative. Columbus brought the pepper back to Spain, and popularity for the chilli soon spread like wildfire across Europe.

And then the chilli began to make its way along the trade route to the East, established by the Portuguese in their search for treasures such as gold, silver and spices.

Life on board ship meant days and months of boredom punctuated by times of danger and privation. Disease, especially on long voyages, was widespread – scurvy being the most common complaint. There was some understanding that fruit prevented it, but often this was not an option. Of course, chillies are rich in Vitamin C. While it was known at the time that they prevented scurvy and they were eaten to stave this off, they were not readily available at sea.

To die of scurvy was an excruciating experience. The gums of these poor people swelled up, their teeth fell out, fever and hallucinations set in and wounds appeared on their bloated legs. In stark contrast, the ship's captain would feast on eggs, ham, cheeses, rolls with fresh butter and all-important fruit and vegetables. Although as an interminable voyage progressed, he too would begin to suffer.

Now, of course, these intrepid explorers had to stop en route to replenish their supplies. So the Portuguese began to set up trading posts and forts along their way around Africa. These became bustling little communities and regular ports of call for the boatloads of explorers passing through on their way to India.

Later traders and prospectors penetrated the interior regions, searching for gold. How much gold they found isn't clear, but we do know that they found another precious commodity – Peri-Peri.

The warm soil and humid climate of south-east Africa were ideal growing conditions for Peri-Peri and it was the local Swahili people who introduced the Portuguese to it. The African Bird's Eye Chilli was known variously as Piri-Piri, Peli-Peli or Peri-Peri, all Swahili variations resulting from different tribal pronunciations of l and r. Everyone was so overwhelmed by this fiery little chilli and its positive effect on life that no one could agree on how to say it.

The local African people showed the Portuguese how much more pleasure they could derive from their food – and from life in general – by simply using this one rather magical ingredient in their cooking.

Soon, Peri-Peri plants were sprouting up in the gardens of Portuguese settlements across south-east Africa. Little birds, attracted by the bright colours of Peri-Peri, loved their taste as much as the Portuguese did. The birds' droppings would fall wherever they flew, and soon most of south-east Africa was alive with Peri-Peri plants.

taxonomy

Kingdom: Plantae

Division: Magnoliophyta

Class: Magnoliopsida

Order: Solanales

Family: Solanaceae

Genus: *Capsicum*

Species: *Frutescens*

Pod type: Bell

Cultivar: Oriole

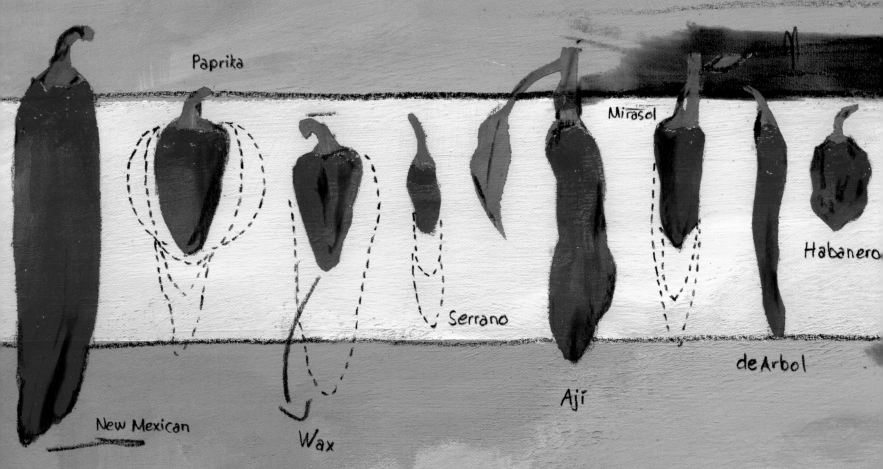

Paprika

Mirasol

Habanero

Serrano

Aji

de Arbol

New Mexican

Wax

It is generally accepted by the people whose job it is to know these things, that there are about 27 *Capsicum* species distributed across the world. It belongs to the Solanaceae – or nightshade – family, which includes tomatoes, potatoes, aubergines, petunias and tobacco.

Of those 27 species, 22 are wild and 5 domesticated: *Capsicum annuum*, *Capsicum baccatum*, *Capsicum chinense*, *Capsicum frutescens* and *Capsicum pubescens*. Now you have an interesting topic of conversation to dine out on.

58

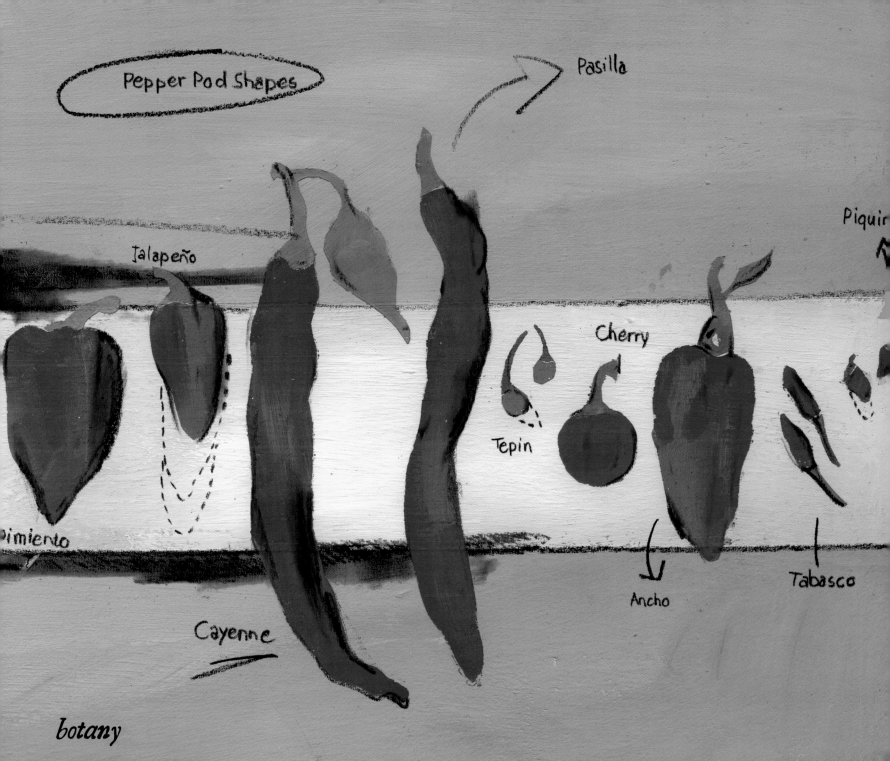

Pepper Pod Shapes

Pasilla

Jalapeño

Piquir

Cherry

Tepin

Pimiento

Cayenne

Ancho

Tabasco

botany

In botanical terms, chillies are berries, although horticulturists consider them to be a fruit. If chillies are harvested green, they are called vegetables, but when dried or harvested ripe, they are called a spice. Talk about having an identity crisis. If a chilli were a person, it would be the sort of person who tells you, with a wink, *I can be whatever you want me to be.*

leaves

Peri-Peri plants are perennial and can reach a maximum height of about a metre. Their leaves range from 5mm to 120mm in length and are egg-like in shape.

flowers

The petals of the Peri-Peri flower are usually white. The flowers are 'perfect', meaning they possess male and female sexual organs. Chillies cross-pollinate easily, which is why there are so many varieties.

pods

Most pods are ripe for picking after about 70 days. When picking, the pod should be pinched and pulled gently from the calyx. If the pod is pinched too hard, sugars are released. This causes bruising and means that black marks will appear during the drying process. Pods left to partially dry on the stem before picking end up with a better, richer colour than those that are picked when ripe.

the plant

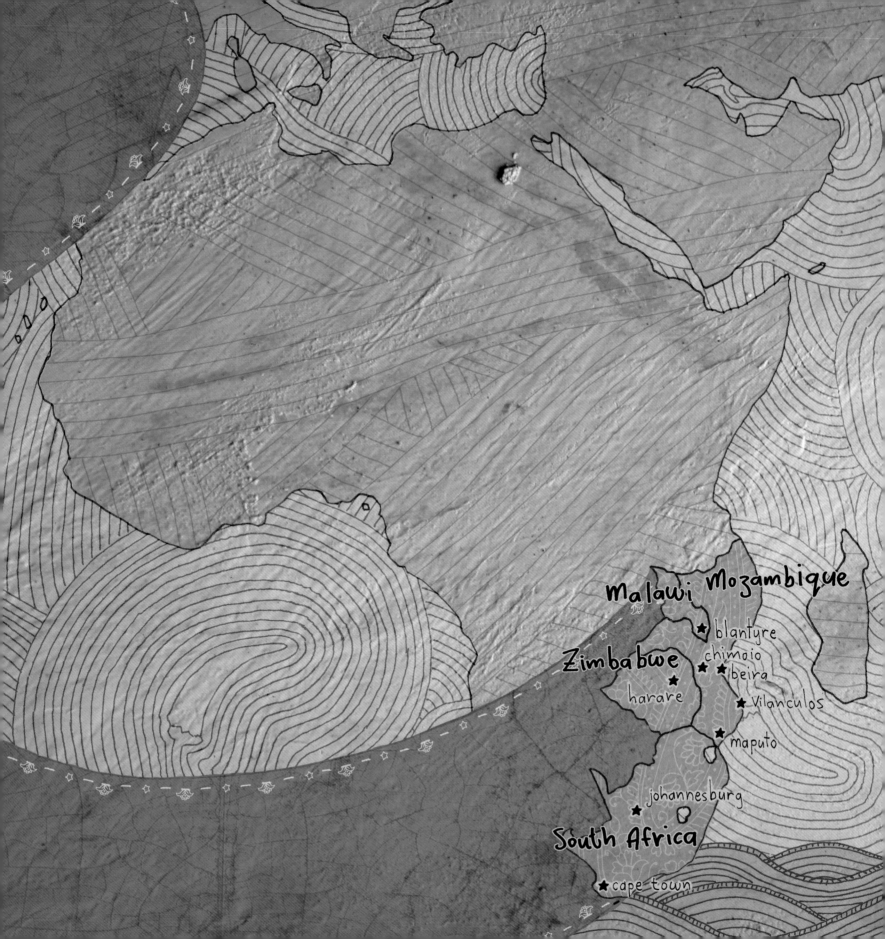

Malawi Mozambique

★ blantyre

Zimbabwe chimoio
★ beira

harare ★

★ Vilanculos

★ maputo

johannesburg
★

South Africa

★ cape town

Peri-Peri plants grow wild all over Mozambique, because its climate is ideal. Peri-Peri is most famous for being the main ingredient in Peri-Peri sauce, and Mozambique is acknowledged as being the home of Peri-Peri sauce. Mozambique was of course a Portuguese colony. First explored by Vasco da Gama in about 1498, it had been colonised by Portugal by 1505.

the source of flavour

Just about every family of Portuguese descent in Mozambique has a recipe that has been handed down to them. Although not a complicated recipe, there are countless variations. In its simplest form, Peri-Peri chillies are crushed and blended with fresh lemon juice, olive oil, vinegar, a hint of garlic and coarse sea salt. To learn more about Peri-Peri – where it comes from, what it is, exactly – a visit to Mozambique is required...

BEM VINDO
CHINZUNCA

E DE MOÇAMBIQUE

BEIRA

journey

beira

Beira is the second largest town in Mozambique after the capital Maputo. At sea level, it largely comprises reclaimed land, and its atmosphere is damp. A population of an estimated half a million people live here, and it is home to the busiest port in Mozambique.

The port of Beira is the main port for the central parts of the country, as well as for the landlocked countries of Zimbabwe, Zambia and Malawi that border on Mozambique.

The Frelimo party has been in power since the early 1970s, but was engaged in two decades of civil war with Renamo. The civil war ended in 1995, but its consequences are still very much in evidence.

"Of course, every cook in Mozambique
has his own particular way of preparing Piri-Piri."
Sir Laurens van der Post

Frankut, set close to the beach, is proudly declared by the locals as the best seafood restaurant in Mozambique. It is run by Anselmo Inocêncio and his wife, Francisca.

Frankut is a loose collection of straw-walled rooms with polished concrete floors, a bar at the front, the restaurant to the right, an arrangement of seven or eight tables with plastic tablecloths. Without walls, the sound of the ocean is an undercurrent to conversation, the chilled half-litre brown bottles of Manica beer knocked back to fend off the heat.

The kitchen is around the back. The pots and pans are stacked on shelves outside the restaurant and the stainless steel counters in the kitchen are set on trestles and scrubbed clean. Inocêncio stands in front of an ancient barbeque made from half an oil drum set outside the kitchen, where he cooks in the dim glow of the electric light from inside.

82

Inocêncio makes his own simple Peri-Peri sauce, a blend of finely chopped fresh chillies, lemon juice and salt. Arranged on the barbeque he has calamari, big prawns, bream and other local line fish. And where does he get his fish from? He gestures towards the beach. From the sea, he says, without a trace of irony.

He grills the seafood clamped in griddles over hot coals, basting them with lemon juice, butter and garlic. The seafood is piled onto platters. The meat in the prawns pulls easily from the shell. Daubed in Peri-Peri sauce, they are tender and moist. The Peri-Peri is at first sweet. Then the burn hits the back of your tongue and, creeping all the way down your throat, lingers.

Crabs can be found all over Beira and they are a treat – juicy and full of flavour. The calamari steaks are slightly charred but tender, the line fish fresh and salty.

Sardinhas (sardines) are caught just off the coast and dried in piles on the beach.

These are then sold inland, and usually prepared with Peri-Peri sauce and served with rice.

Down a long dirt road in the town of Gondola sits Mokombo, a new Peri-Peri farm being set up in virgin soil.

gondola

While still involved in stripping the natural vegetation, laying seed beds and setting up irrigation, the farmers' long-term plan is to grow sugarcane and produce ethanol. To get started, though, they intend to grow a few cash crops, like tomatoes – and Peri-Peri. The seeds will flower and fruit for three years. After that new seeds will have to be purchased and planted for a new crop.

Growing behind one of the outbuildings of the farmhouse is a clump of wild Peri-Peri bushes. These are really tiny African Bird's Eye Chillies, less than a centimetre in length. Bite into one: it's full of flavour and incredibly hot.

Locally-grown Peri-Peri for sale
at a market in Manica.
The plant thrives in this hilly,
humid region.

manica

Sixteen kilometres from the border with Zimbabwe, Manica is a rural area where subsistence farming is how most of its inhabitants make a living. There is a small market on the outskirts of the town. Up the mountain to where many chilli farms lie, there are differing styles of architecture. Brick houses stand side by side with thatched mud huts and homes made from clay bricks. Several hundred concrete steps lead up to the doorway of a beautiful dirty-white church which stands proudly on the crest of a small hill.

Mofati Burakufisi with his three wives and their many children tend the Peri-Peri fields.

One of the Peri-Peri fields measures about 2 000 square metres in a shape that follows the curvature of the hill. Muddy water flows along an irrigation ditch dug along the edge of the field. A rooster sprints through the rows of chilli plants. A hen pecks at the soil, her chicks waddling in a group behind her.

It is a bright, hot day. Slight wisps of cloud smear the pale blue sky. In the sharp light, the plants look healthy and are growing a dark green. The chillies are pale, verging on orange, something to do with the red soil, which is rich in nitrogen and oxygen.

A half-hour drive away, near Bellis, is a second farm, across railway tracks and on a road that runs beside a row of derelict railway houses. A kind-faced man is tending his crop.

There is a white ant problem in this chilli field. Several plants were being attacked. The advice given was to remove the afflicted plants and replace the root with a stick, up which the ants would run rather than migrate to a nearby plant.

Usually the yield of this farm is very high. The health and fertility of this crop is attributed to the natural spring water that runs from the mountains rather than the hard work and dedication of the farmer and his family. In the roughly made furrows built by the owner and other local farmers, the water is clear and bracingly cold. It gushes in great volume all the way along the road past the farm and to the other farms nearby.

Far left: Charles is an agronomist who travels from region to region, helping Peri-Peri farmers solve problems and improve crop yield.

vilanculos

Vilanculos is a tiny resort town in the south of Mozambique. The beach is a long stretch of white sand. High tide means that the beach reaches far out into the sea. Sometimes it looks as if it reaches all the way across to the Bazaruto Archipelago.

Clockwise from left: now a bank, this building was originally the home of Joaquin Alves and his wife, Dona Ana, who made the legendary Peri-Peri sauce that everyone in Mozambique knows; the Dona Ana Hotel was built by Alves in honour of his wife; the hotel overlooks the Vilanculos harbour and has been in a state of disrepair for more than a decade.

In the 1950s and 60s, Joaquim Alves, a flamboyant Portuguese businessman, began to develop Vilanculos and the Bazaruto Archipelago for tourism. He centered his efforts on the island of Santa Carolina (or Paradise Island) and constructed a hotel there. According to local legend, Alves made his fortune during the Second World War by supplying diesel to passing fleets of German U-boats preying on Allied shipping in the Indian Ocean. Allegedly there still exists the secret pipeline in the channel used by Alves and his accomplices to deliver the diesel to the submarines. In the Vilanculos harbour at the northern end of town is another hotel Alves built, the Dona Ana.

Dona Ana – his wife – was famous for the Peri-Peri sauce she made, based on a recipe passed down to her from her grandmother. For two decades, her major-domo was a man called Joaquim Fernando Huate. She trusted him implicitly and he, in turn, was loyal to her all of her life. Fernando was a helper in the kitchen of one of her husband's hotels, when he was spotted by Dona Ana. She taught him her Peri-Peri recipe and he continues to make it to this day.

Fernando Huate who looks to be in his late sixties, is a soft-spoken, considered man with enormous dignity. The Alves's home is now the BIM Expresso bank building. Dona Ana's kitchen was in the basement, where she taught him her recipe for Peri-Peri sauce. This recipe has no oil: it is made of lemon juice, salt and chillies strained and then left in the sun to ferment. When it starts to bubble, it is deemed ready.

Right: Joaquim Fernando Huate.
Overleaf Left: Fernando holds up a photograph of his one-time employer's husband.
Overleaf Centre: Joaquim Alves, flanked by two unidentified men.

The label gummed to the bottles of Fernando's Peri-Peri sauce is simply done — a square of white paper with neat purple capital letters on it that says:

MOLHO DE PIRI PIRI	*Peri-Peri sauce*
PREPARADO POR	*made by*
FERNANDO HUATE	*Fernando Huate*
TIPO DONA ANA	*in remembrance*
LEMBRANÇA DE	*of Dona Ana*
VILANCULOS	*Vilanculos*
MOÇAMBIQUE	*Mozambique*

Because he wants to honour her memory and all that she did for him, he named the sauce he sells after its creator. The Peri-Peri chillies he uses come from small farms outside Vilanculos. He sends word in advance to several famers with details of how much chilli he needs. When he arrives, they will have his order ready for him. Fernando wears goggles to protect his eyes when he makes his sauce, gloves to protect his hands and an apron to protect his clothes.

Four samples of molho de Piri-Piri, or Peri-Peri sauce,
from restaurants or vendors in various places across Mozambique.

nature & *nurture*

Left to nature, Peri-Peri will quite happily grow to be healthy and hot. But nurture the plant in your garden, and it will thrive and provide you with more chillies than you could possibly need.

Peri-Peri is filled with goodness. Eat just enough and it has a nurturing effect on your body.

A great contradiction of Peri-Peri is that it is an irritant, but at the same time has long been reputed to have healing qualities. Its uses have been far-reaching and often peculiar. The medicinal use of chillies dates back to the Mayans who used them to treat asthma, coughs and sore throats. The Aztecs eased toothache with chillies.

A Spanish doctor writing in the 1570s attributed many curative properties to the chilli: "It dooeth dissolve windes, it is good for the breaste and for theim that bee colde of complexion: it doeth heale and comforte, strengthenyng the principal members."

The Portuguese had introduced chillies to South India. By the 19th Century, physicians there were prescribing chilli soups to treat cholera. While it must have made for a delicious meal, it seems doubtful that it could have been in any way helpful.

In Africa, rumour had it that red (but not green) chillies held the secret to eternal youth and, weirdly, that they would cure haemorrhoids.

Modern-day pharmaceutical companies use Capsaicin as an ingredient in soothing balms. Anyone who has chopped a chilli without using gloves and then touched his or her face, will know the odd numbing sensation that sets in at the same time as the pain. Creams with Capsaicin as an ingredient are used to treat neuralgia, a painful nerve disorder that often occurs after a case of shingles. Capsaicin has qualities as an anticoagulant, which means that it could contribute to preventing strokes.

There is a heated debate as to whether eating chillies soothes arthritic pain. Some say chillies intensify inflammation, others that it lessens it. However, there does seem to be a link between the two. A group of American scientists reported findings that the pain people feel when eating chillies stimulates the same chemical signals in the body that the pain of arthritis does. A protein called TRPVI sends a message to the brain and triggers pain. The way this protein works is controlled by a molecule. By blocking this molecule, the scientist reasoned that they could stop arthritis sufferers experiencing pain.

The anti-bacterial properties of chilli also mean that, when used in combination with thyme and lavender, it can be gargled to ease a sore throat.

medicinal values

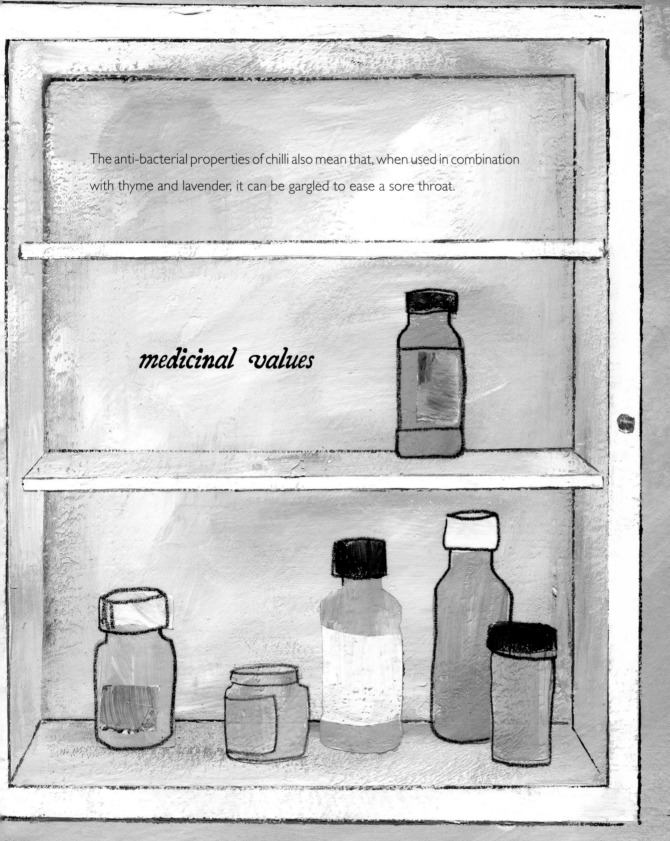

It is said that the chilli has addictive qualities. It can safely be considered a healthy addiction because it has a beneficial effect on the body. Green chillies are particularly high in Vitamin C, with twice the content of any citrus fruit. Not only that, but all chillies promote growth and tissue repair.

health

Chilli is an excellent purifying agent and a tremendous source of Vitamin A. Dried red chillies actually contain more Vitamin A than fresh carrots. If a chilli is dried, its Vitamin A content is concentrated. This increase is because of a rise in carotene during the drying process. It is in fact the carotene that causes chillies to be red in colour. Vitamin A is a resilient little vitamin and doesn't break down over time or when heated.

The list of vitamins and minerals contained in a chilli goes on:
Thymine (Vitamin B1), Riboflavin (Vitamin B2), Niacin (Vitamin B3), Folic acid (Vitamin B12), Potassium, Phosphorus, Iron and Calcium.

The B Vitamins are good for both your metabolism and immune system and help to prevent anaemia by promoting growth and division of red blood cells. Potassium aids in maintaining the balance of electrolytes in your body and can contribute to reducing hypertension. The phosphorus, iron and calcium all help build strong bones and contribute to keeping teeth healthy (which goes some way to explaining why chilli lovers find it so easy to smile unselfconsciously after eating a spicy meal).

Chillies are also antioxidants, which assist in cancelling out the cell-damaging effects of free radicals. People who eat fruits and vegetables rich in antioxidant compounds, such as polyphenols and anthocyanins, have a lower risk of developing some cancers, heart disease and other neurological diseases.

Chillies are a must for health-conscious eaters as they contain no fat, are very high in dietary fibre and have a very low kilojoule count. Capsaicin is a natural antibiotic that slows the growth of bacteria in the body and in food products. This explains why spicy foods are likely to be less perishable.

The chilli is known to lower cholesterol levels. It increases blood flow, stimulates the appetite and speeds up the metabolism. With it doing so much, no wonder it can make people sweat.

HOW TO GROW chillies

Peri-Peri seeds should be sown as early in the spring as possible. That way, they can be out in the garden during the height of summer when the sun is at its hottest.

home-grown

If you live somewhere that has a cooler climate than the tropical east coast of Africa where chillies are normally grown, seedlings should be placed in trays in a greenhouse. Warm, well-drained loam is recommended. Ideally, the soil should be kept at a temperature of about 25°C (77°F). Even in a warm climate, it's a good idea to have the sprouting seedlings on a windowsill, in full view of the sun.

yes!!
I have
The chilli

They should be transplanted to the garden eight weeks later. Leave a space of one metre between rows of plants and about 300 millimetres between each plant. This will allow them to reach their optimal height.

Flowering usually occurs about three months after sowing. The plants will continue to flower for another three months after that. This may last longer in a warmer climate. Sun and water are what Peri-Peri plants love most. They will, however, need protection from winds and pests.

Harvesting should take place in hot, dry weather, during late summer. Only mature Peri-Peri chillies should be picked. The fruit will not ripen if picked green. Achieving full flavour and delightful heat only happens on the plant. Peri-Peri picked too early will not have had time to develop any real pungency. The pungency of a chilli is increased by the amount of environmental stress (extreme heat, for example) to which it is subjected. Even a short period of very hot weather, for instance, will increase a chilli's Capsaicin content.

When picking Peri-Peri, those with glossy skins that are firm to the touch are the ones to choose. If it comes off the stem easily, it is ready. If it is tugged on and does not come free, give it a few more days. Leave it to Peri-Peri: it knows when it's ready to give itself up to the kitchen.

Peri-Peri plants can be harvested up to six times during the summer. Picking actually stimulates the plants to produce more flowers and in turn, more chillies – which is, after all, what we are after.

Peri-Peri chillies kept in a sealed container in the refrigerator should stay fresh for about two weeks. But it's doubtful they'll last even that long if anyone else knows they're in there.

Keep a few ripe ones for next year's crop. Hang them in a dry atmosphere and then when dried out, collect all the seeds and seal them in an envelope. Label it and keep in a cool, dry place for next spring.

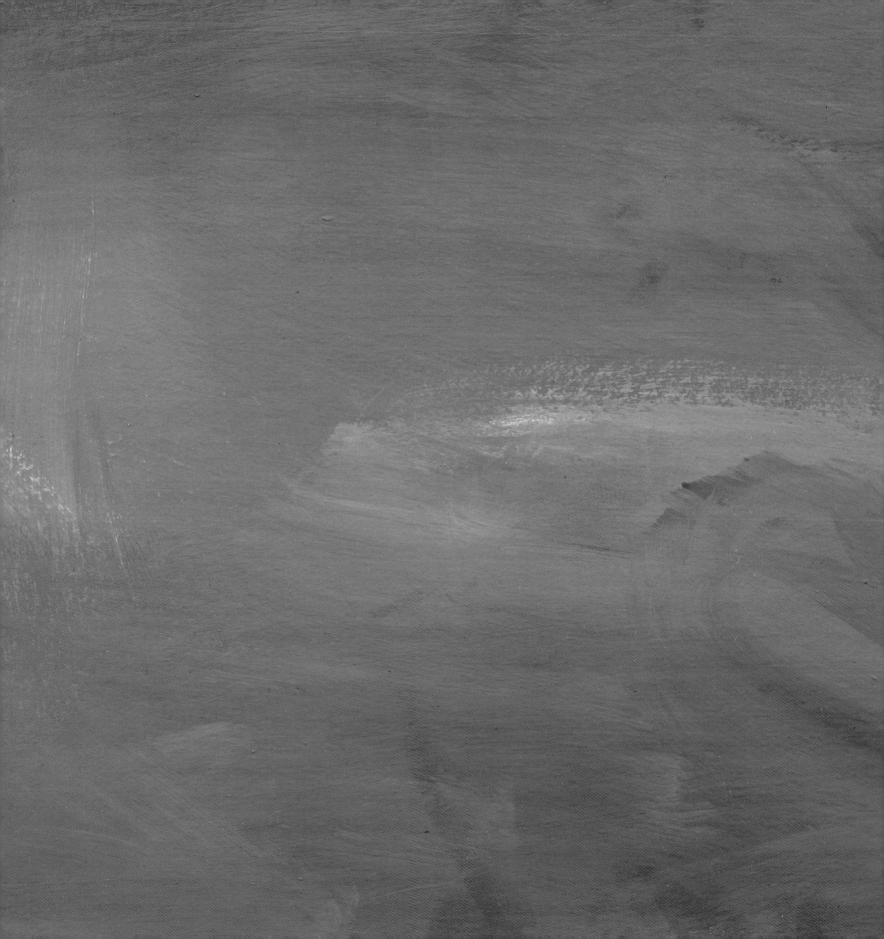

sex & the senses

Consuming Peri-Peri is always breathtaking. It excites your senses with a power that no other ingredient can rival.
In fact, it's an experience that can be so intense that it has become associated in people's minds
with that other life-affirming and passionate act: sex.

anatomy

As Peri-Peri grows and ripens, it proves itself as the most sensual of all chillies by standing erect on the stem, aiming itself at the sun's light and heat. Its phallic appearance while it grows hints not-so-subtly at its rumoured qualities as an aphrodisiac and at its long association with love and sex.

Other chillies tend to hang down like fruit. There is something inherently masculine about Peri-Peri pods as they lasciviously follow the sun as if she is an especially voluptuous woman passing by in an exaggeratedly slow arc.

But Peri-Peri isn't all man. It has a certain womanly attribute too. When one is cut open, it becomes distinctly feminine. A cross-section of a chilli could almost be a diagrammatic representation of the female reproductive organs.

sex

Peri-Peri is native to warm climates. There is always the subtle suggestion of sexiness in hot countries. It's something in the warm atmosphere, the near-constant sweatiness of a humid climate and the pleasure one takes in the feeling of the sunshine on one's skin. One has only to think of the rhythms of the tropics and the myriad dances which have developed there.

That stirring sensation you feel when eating a chilli is felt by everyone, no matter what the physical reaction. Whenever you eat Peri-Peri, you want more of it immediately.

Many people say that eating chocolate causes a similar physical response. When you eat chocolate, Serotonin is released in the brain, producing feelings of pleasure. When you eat Peri-Peri, the ecstasy produced is more intense, and you have the very apparent physical signs to prove it. When you feel Peri-Peri's burn, the pain receptors in the nose, mouth and stomach release Substance P, a neurotransmitter – or messenger – whose function it is to inform the brain of pain or irritation. Substance P triggers the brain to release endorphins. Endorphins are natural painkillers that affect people in a manner similar to morphine, inducing an enveloping sense of contentment. Capsaicin has been shown to reduce the levels of Substance P, which is why people who repeatedly eat Peri-Peri need more and more to feel the burn.

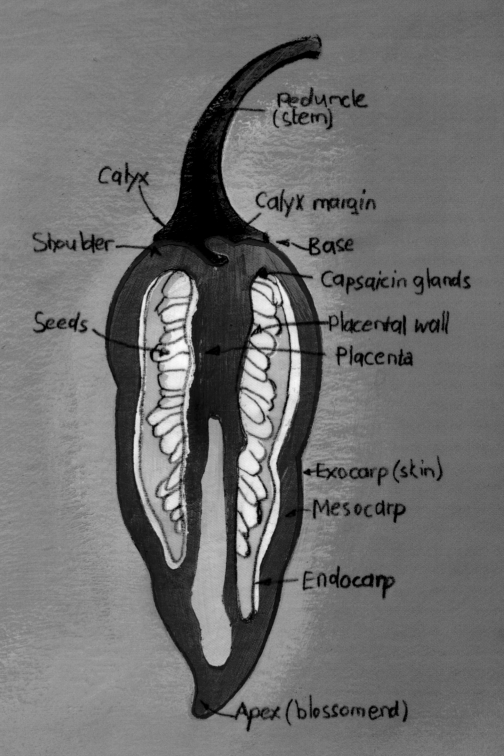

Peduncle (stem)

Calyx

Calyx margin

Shoulder

Base

Capsaicin glands

Seeds

Placental wall

Placenta

Exocarp (skin)

Mesocarp

Endocarp

Apex (blossom end)

Anatomy

On the subject of burn, it is always recommended that men in particular use gloves when chopping chillies. And if they don't, they should forget about going to the men's room for a few hours, unless it is possible for them to relieve themselves without using their hands. There's a certain part of your body that should never ever feel the burn of a chilli. Having said that, a book called *A le paradis sexuel des aphrodisiaques*, written as recently as 1971 actually includes a suggestion to apply ground chilli to the penis prior to sex. It's described as 'extremely erogenous for the woman'. One imagines it could only result in two people doubled over in agony on opposite sides of the bed and someone being asked to spend the night on the sofa.

As discussed earlier, chillies are a stimulant and their uplifting effect is why they are considered an aphrodisiac. The more sensible among us would say that food is only an aphrodisiac if you are sharing a meal with someone special, but it cannot be disputed that a romantic meal prepared with chillies will set the heart racing. It has been suggested that the sweat of someone who has been eating chilli is wildly alluring, which might have something to do with it too.

It wasn't for nothing that a 16th-century Jesuit priest, José de Acosta, said of chillies that they were "prejudicial to the health of young folks, chiefly to the soul, for it provokes to lust".

Paradoxically, chillies have also been used to fend off indecent thoughts. It is said that if a young Aztec girl stared inappropriately at a man, her mother would rub her eyes with chilli as punishment. A conclusion we could draw from this is that as well as 'provoking to lust', chilli has also been used as a contraceptive. A poor Aztec girl subjected to that could hardly want to glance longingly at a man ever again, let alone entertain thoughts of being with him.

And how does the food of love itself reproduce?

At those times of the year when a young male bird's fancy turns to love, he will find that he craves carotene, because this enhances the beauty of his plumage, making him more attractive to the opposite sex.

reproduction

In one of nature's ingenious evolutionary workings, the heat of chillies does not affect birds. Chillies need them to propagate their seeds far and wide as they fly. Mammals are an ineffective vehicle for seed dispersal, which is why it was nature's intention that we don't enjoy chillies. Nature obviously didn't anticipate that we would take a perverse pleasure in pain.

Birds will select their chillies, like we humans might at a market stall, for firmness and ripeness. They then flutter up to the high branches of trees to enjoy them. The chilli seeds fall to the ground where they can begin the process of germination, either immediately as the birds fight over the especially juicy ones or later on in their droppings. The stomach acid of birds cannot digest the seeds.

Nature's decision to make chillies pungent was so that we, apparently being no good at dispersing its seeds, would be deterred from eating them. But perhaps it isn't an accident of nature that we humans ended up finding chillies so delightful, because we must have propagated more of them than all the birds in history put together. Our avid love affair with the chilli has meant that the *Capsicum* family has grown bigger than the very first chilli plant could ever possibly have imagined.

Eating Peri-Peri is an unrivalled sensory experience. Strangely, there are people in the world who aren't keen on hot food and don't like Peri-Peri. It should be pointed out to people like this, that they might be missing out on the most blissful experience you can have. (Or the second most blissful experience you can have.)

the sensory pleasures of Peri-Peri

As mentioned earlier, the beautifully vivid red colour of a chilli is caused by carotene, or specifically, the carotenoids or organic pigments that carotene contains. Chilli is used as a colourant in foods, drugs and cosmetics and even to enhance the colours of koi fish in aquariums and the tail feathers of captive flamingos. Of course, you don't need to know this to appreciate the brilliant colour of a chilli any more than you need to know the biography of an artist to appreciate one of his paintings.

The chilli has been a source of inspiration for making noise of a musical kind, too. Early jazz of the 1920s defied Western musical traditions. Instead of musicians playing music as it was written by a composer, songs became a starting point around which they would improvise. This was known as 'hot' music. A pianist with the unlikely name of Jelly Roll Morton put together a group called the Red Hot Peppers and recorded some of the finest performances in this style. Listening to this music now makes for difficult listening if your ears aren't attuned to it. It's rough and ready, but there is vitality and a sense of excitement present that is almost unrivalled in modern music. This is the kind of aural equivalent of the energy and pleasure elicited by chillies in food.

In a contemporary example of music and chillies crossing paths, we look to the Red Hot Chili Peppers, initially infamous for several members' addictions to a substance slightly more dangerous than Capsaicin.

"Hot tamales and they're red hot, yes she got 'em for sale"
Robert Johnson, They're Red Hot

In the legendary blues man's song, you know we aren't really being told about a woman's cooking skills. Tamales are a Mexican dish made of crushed chillies with chopped meat, seasoned, wrapped in cornhusks and then steamed. Chillies might very well rival music as the food of love. It's no coincidence that when you find someone physically attractive, you say that they're hot. And if you're in the company of someone you think is hot, you'll feel hot yourself.

I must eat more peri-peri
I must eat more peri-peri
I must eat more peri-peri
I must eat more peri-peri

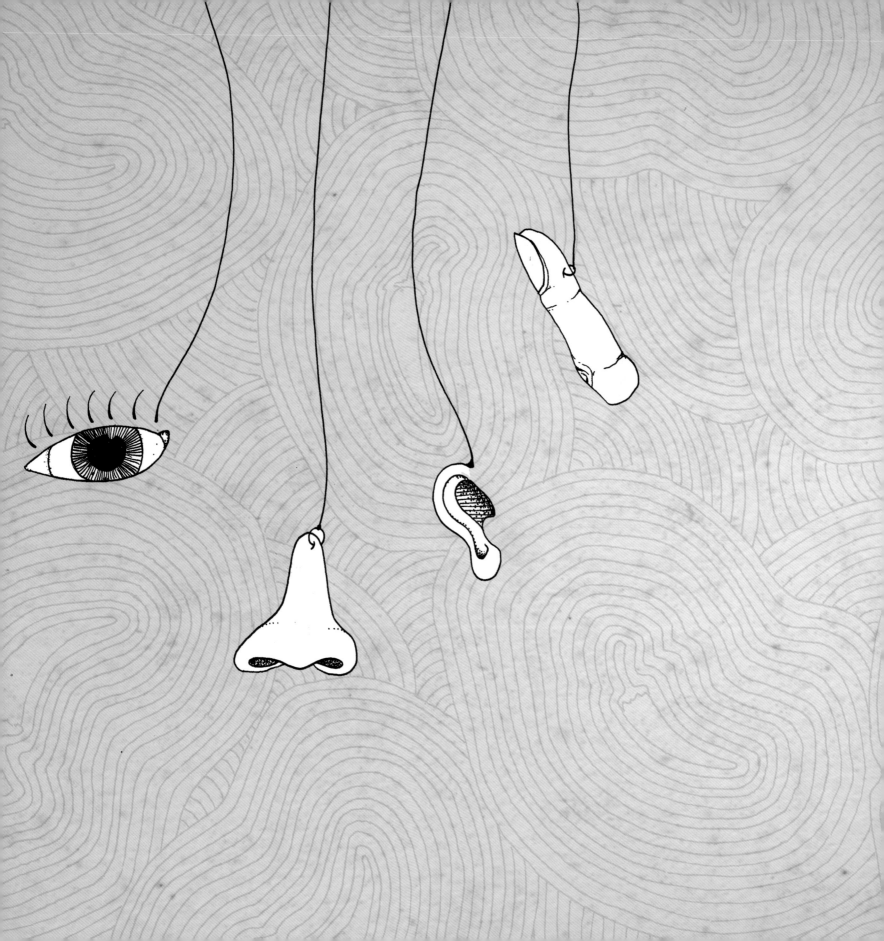

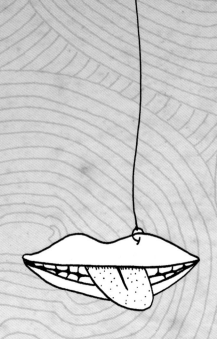

To cook with and eat Peri-Peri is to have all five of your senses stirred. This is an experience we wish to echo here. It will take the form of an imaginative exercise.

firing up the senses

Let's imagine that it's early in the evening. You're standing at the kitchen counter, about to prepare something delicious for your family or for some friends. It really doesn't matter who – all that's important is that they are your very favourite people. It's a summer day (the windows are open). The counter is cold, but it soon warms to your touch. A voice is coming from the radio, but the volume is low so you can't make out what is being said. You have rubbed down with salt and pepper a plump roasting chicken and it is now in a baking tray on the stove top, ready for the oven. Your hands are greasy and gritty with seasoning and olive oil.

You are now ready to make your Peri-Peri sauce with which to baste the chicken. Set out on a chopping board you have a small cup of lemon juice, and garlic, some salt, olive oil, oregano and paprika.

On the counter is a white ceramic bowl, which contains a handful of red and green Peri-Peri chillies. You have picked them yourself from the plant growing in a pot outside your kitchen window and you feel a mild sense of parental affection for them. There's something irresistible about them. You pluck a green one from the bowl…

You have in your fingers a small, firm Peri-Peri pod. It is deep emerald in colour, so green it almost looks synthetic. Not much bigger than the top of your little finger, from the last joint to the tip, this chilli is so adorably small that it could have been made from plastic – a toy you'd find in a Christmas cracker.

sight

Green is a colour one would associate with safety and health. Imagine the surprise of the first person to bite into what must have appeared to be a sweet berry.

The other Peri-Peri chilli you have taken from the bowl is green's complementary colour and the internationally accepted colour for danger – red. You know where you stand with something coloured bright fire-engine red.

Red is also the colour that rises in the cheeks of someone enjoying a meal rich in Peri-Peri. His eyes water as if touched by deeply felt emotion. He will mop at his face as if in the grip of a bout of laughter, the kind of laughter that comes from deep down in his belly. Seeing his face is a joy to behold, especially if you are the person who has prepared the meal he is eating.

Fresh Peri-Peri is always small and firm to the touch. Its red skin is smooth and has a healthy shine to it, like the skin of any fresh, ripe fruit.

touch

As you roll it around between your fingers, there is something about it that tempts you to eat it. This might be because it is so satisfyingly small and neat looking. Perhaps it is the succulence that you can sense lies within. Just from looking at it, you wouldn't expect it to be quite so explosive on the tongue.

People suggest that you wear kitchen gloves to protect your skin when chopping chillies. That way, if you rub your eyes or nose later on, you don't find yourself in agony. But, for the purposes of this sensory exploration, let's leave the gloves off. It will be far more intimate this way. If you have especially sensitive skin, however, it is probably a better idea to keep them on.

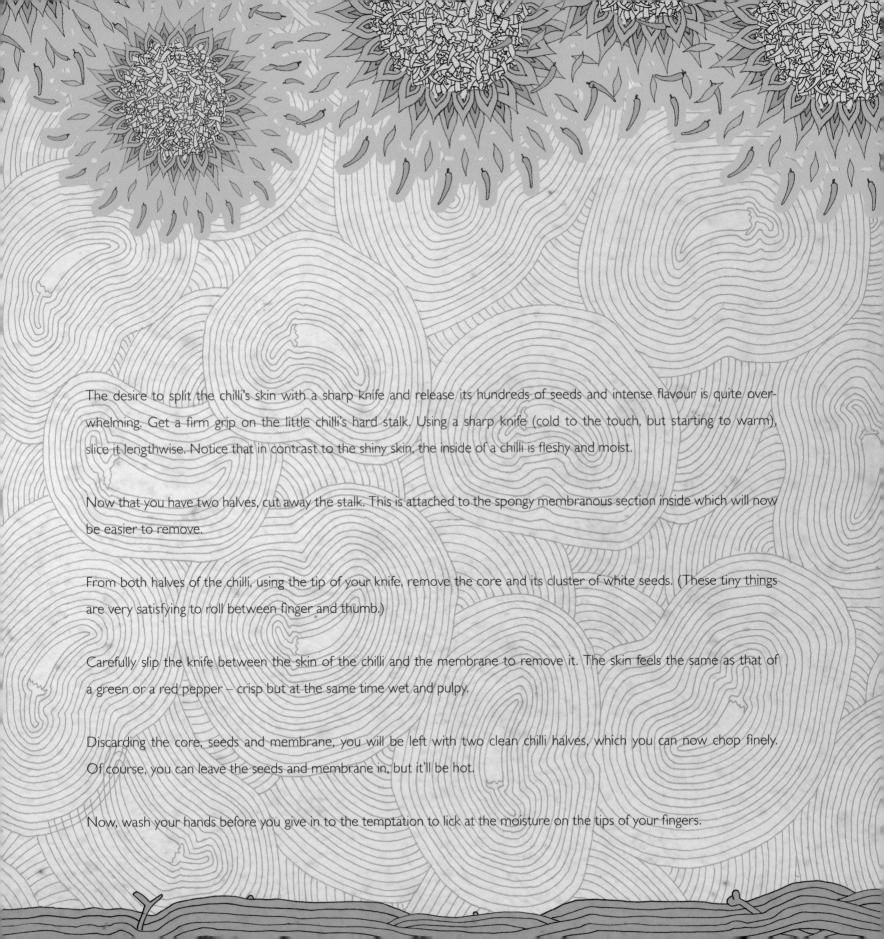

The desire to split the chilli's skin with a sharp knife and release its hundreds of seeds and intense flavour is quite over-whelming. Get a firm grip on the little chilli's hard stalk. Using a sharp knife (cold to the touch, but starting to warm), slice it lengthwise. Notice that in contrast to the shiny skin, the inside of a chilli is fleshy and moist.

Now that you have two halves, cut away the stalk. This is attached to the spongy membranous section inside which will now be easier to remove.

From both halves of the chilli, using the tip of your knife, remove the core and its cluster of white seeds. (These tiny things are very satisfying to roll between finger and thumb.)

Carefully slip the knife between the skin of the chilli and the membrane to remove it. The skin feels the same as that of a green or a red pepper – crisp but at the same time wet and pulpy.

Discarding the core, seeds and membrane, you will be left with two clean chilli halves, which you can now chop finely. Of course, you can leave the seeds and membrane in, but it'll be hot.

Now, wash your hands before you give in to the temptation to lick at the moisture on the tips of your fingers.

People often consider smell to be the most evocative sense. A familiar smell can transport us through space and time. Where will Peri-Peri take you? Lift the little Peri-Peri chilli to your nose – not too closely as you don't want to irritate the sensitive skin around your nostrils. Give it a gentle sniff. You might not smell anything at first. So roll it around in your fingers, warm it up a little to get it going. Now try again. Give it another sniff. What do you smell? If your nostrils are really sensitive, you'll be able to detect several aromas – not only one.

smell

You can guess how hot it is going to be simply by smelling it. First, there's the fresh wet scent of green pepper, which might remind you of a freshly mowed lawn, summer and eating outdoors. Then there is a defined fruitiness which gives way to a smell that is both sharp and subtle. This is the chilli's piquancy, its heat.

What does that heat bring to mind? Cooking with your family as a child, perhaps. Or a far-off tropical country that you once visited.

Finally, the heat gives way to delicate mustiness like tobacco leaves, fresh yet smoky. It's a 'green' smell, although there's a darker undertone to it too. Where does your mind drift to? Maybe there was once a garden you played in that had the same smell.

You wouldn't think that so many different smells would be present in a single chilli. Smells are made up of other aromas: atoms make up molecules, which are what we smell. And these smells, in turn, make up more complex aromas. It's like the bouquet of aromas that develop with age in a fine wine. "Smell is our chemical sense," writes Luca Turin in his *The Secret of Scent,* "and we are so used to it that we do not stop to think how amazing it is". And nor have you considered before how amazing the African Bird's Eye Chilli in your hand is.

The temptation to bite into the little chilli in your hand is there. Just the tip, you think. That won't hurt at all. Peri-Peri might look innocent enough, but don't be fooled. Everyone knows someone, their father or an uncle, perhaps – it's almost always a man – who by preference and a desire to impress, will eat a Peri-Peri whole. This is not the ideal way to experience Peri-Peri, as it seems unlikely that this makes the most of what it has to offer. Do not try this at home.

taste

All the physical effects of Peri-Peri are exacerbated by eating too much of it, but having said that, there are far more pleasurable ways of consuming it. A little goes a long way and there is perhaps more joy to be had in using it in small amounts than to submit to sensory overload and eating a whole lot in one go.

For the sake of experience, let's try the tip. Bite into the tight flesh of the chilli and feel a numbing tingle on your tongue. Roll it around your mouth and the anaesthesia spreads. Then you'll start to sense a growing warmth work its way along your tongue and your lips. Now swallow and have the same sensations chase the chilli down your throat.

The effects of Peri-Peri are also physical. The thrilling hint of heat that causes a sharp intake of breath. The prickling of sweat on your upper lip and forehead, your nostrils beginning to dampen. The rush that travels from your mouth, through your delighted body and to your stomach.

While all of this may not sound like a pleasant experience, we all know that there is far more to it than that: there's a thrill that rises with the heat, an exhilaration that takes hold and slowly fades until you have another bite...

We take as much pleasure in the sounds of the kitchen while we cook as we do the dish we end up with.

Above the humming from the radio on your kitchen counter there are other noises that come together like a full orchestra: the rattle and thud of the utensil drawer being opened and closed, the sharp sound of a whisk against the sides of a glass mixing bowl, the gentle sputtering of oil in a pan, the squeaking of onions as they soften and sweeten, the bubbling of sauce in a pot, the tap-dancing of a knife against a wooden board as you chop Peri-Peri into slivers...

hearing

You can hold a chilli up to your ear but it won't, we hope for your sake, make any sound. To understand how chillies affect the fifth and final sense – hearing – you will need to serve to friends and family the meal you have spent your late afternoon and early evening preparing. Murmurs of enjoyment will be heard, followed by exclamations of pleasure and finally, when dinner is over and everyone has got their breath back, requests for the recipe.

recipes & recipes

A recipe is like a good story and Peri-Peri is the embellishment — the little details that make that story
so compelling and so memorable. Peri-Peri is a recipe's magical ingredient.
It arouses your taste buds, opening them up to the flavours in a dish that would ordinarily go unnoticed.

A recipe is like a good story, and peri-peri is the embellishment – the little details that make a story so compelling and so memorable.
Peri-Peri is a recipe's magical ingredient.
Peri-Peri

the storytellers

A book about Peri-Peri simply wouldn't be complete without a selection of Peri-Peri recipes.

Here's your chance to experiment with and enjoy this fiery little chilli.

We asked twenty-four internationally renowned chefs (and all-round hot people) to share their favourite Peri-Peri dishes.

Cass Abrahams Author, well-loved chef and doyenne of Cape Malay cooking, she is no stranger to the wonders of Peri-Peri and uses it often in her cooking. Read her books, *The Cuisine and Culture of the Cape Malays* and *Cass Abrahams Cooks Cape Malay Food from Africa.*

Fausti Airoldi Growing up in a Portuguese family in Mozambique, he learned the secrets of Afro-Portuguese cuisine and cooking with Peri-Peri at home. He lives in Portugal and is chef-patron of the Pragma Fausto Airoldi restaurant in Lisbon.

Coco Fathi Growing up in Zaire where his mother ran the famous restaurant Pili-Pili in Kinshasa, this Burundian-Belgian developed a passion for African flavours and Peri-Peri. He co-authored the internationally award-winning book on African cuisine, *To the Banqueting House – African Cuisine: An Epic Journey.*

Dr Bill Gallagher As a pillar of the South African hotel and tourism industry, and with a lengthy list of achievements that includes Lifelong Honorary President of the World Association of Chefs Societies, he is passionate about sharing the essence of what is authentic southern African cuisine. His knowledge of food and the network that spans the international culinary world is unsurpassable.

Paul Hartmann He is one of the founder members of the South African Chefs Academy. An admired southern African culinary ambassador, he loves cooking with the myriad of unique ingredients found on the African continent.

Mimi Jardim Of Portuguese decent, this South African has taken Portuguese cooking to all four corners of the globe. She has authored a number of well-loved cookbooks including *Cooking the Portuguese Way in South Africa* and *People's Food,* and owns the successful cookery school, Jardim's in Johannesburg, South Africa.

Wilbert Jones His culinary creativity and flair have earned him a place among some of the most creative culinologist in the world. He is the President of Healthy Concepts, Inc., a food and beverage product development and marketing company in Chicago, USA.

Citrum Khumalo Having won several local and international culinary competitions, this proud Zulu has become one of South Africa's most prominent celebrity chefs. His television series *Chef in My Kitchen* taught viewers that it is possible to create magic meals with whatever you have in the kitchen – a philosophy he lives by.

Peter Knipp His extensive international travel and work have made for a unique understanding of cuisines from around the globe. His brilliant culinary talents are now regularly applied in the prestigious *Cuisine & Wine Asia* magazine.

Rudi Liebenberg Executive Chef at The Saxon Hotel in Johannesburg, advisor to the Prue Leith Chefs Academy in Pretoria, South Africa, and South African WINE Magazine's Chef of the Year 2007. Rudi loves experimenting with the unique flavours of Africa and fusing these into culinary delights from across the continent.

Reza Mohammed Colourful, flamboyant chef and restaurateur, Reza Mohammed, runs the Star of India restaurant in London. He hosts the wildly popular television food show Delhi Belly on BBC Food and is the author of *Rice, Spice and all Things Nice*.

Vanie Padayachee Executive Chef at fu.shi in Plettenberg Bay, South Africa, she has worked in the UK as well as in South Africa and was named 'Five Star Chef' in October 2004 by WINE Magazine.

Jodi-Ann Palmer Her experimental and creative approach to food has won her several national and international cooking competitions. She loves cooking with new ingredients, as well as unique ones like Peri-Peri.

Joanina Pastoll and Natalie Bell With a singular talent for what makes a dish delectable, this duo has worked together for many years, as an art director and stylist respectively, on dozens of food photography shoots. Both happily admit to being addicted to Peri-Peri.

Paul Prudhomme He has propelled the cuisine of his native Louisiana into the international spotlight and continues to push the limits by creating exciting American and international dishes. Having used chillies for many years, cooking with Peri-Peri was a real pleasure for him.

Reuben Riffel His restaurant, Reuben's in Franschhoek, South Africa, produces contemporary and classic dishes with an emphasis on simplicity. Within the first year he was declared Chef of the Year; accolades and awards for both the chef-patron and the restaurant have been constant since.

Rochelle Schaetzl Director of the South African Chefs Association and expert on Peri-Peri, she leads the Culinary Innovation team for Nando's Chickenland, an international restaurant group founded in South Africa. The company's famous flame-grilled Peri-Peri chicken recipe has flown around the globe.

Clayton Sherrod Clayton Sherrod is the founder of the Birmingham, Alabama chapter of the American Culinary Federation. He is the recipient of an honorary doctorate from Johnson Wales University, Virginia for his culinary accomplishments.

Stefano Strafella Executive Chef of some of Johannesburg's finest restaurants and previous Principal of the Prue Leith Chefs Academy in Pretoria, award winning South African, Stefano Strafella, has over twenty years of experience in the hospitality industry.

Garth Stroebel As one of the founder members of the South African Chefs Academy and one of South Africa's most experienced and creative chefs, he has earned the reputation of being the father of modern South African cuisine – also the title of his cookbook.

Arnold Tanzer Working in prestigious lodges and restaurants all over Africa not only taught this son of the Netherlands the secrets of authentic African cuisine, but also equipped him for his current role as Continental Director for Africa & the Middle East of the World Association of Chefs Societies. He owns a highly successful catering company, Food on the Move, in Johannesburg, South Africa.

Brian Turner He is one of Britain's most successful chefs. In addition to running highly respected restaurants there, he is also a well-loved television personality, appearing regularly on *Ready Steady Cook*, *This Morning*, *Saturday Cooks* and *Saturday Kitchen* on BBC Food.

Topsi Venter Over the past two decades, she has established a reputation as the *grande dame* of South African cuisine. Her Cape restaurant, Topsi & Co in the beautiful Franschhoek Valley is famous for its honest homestyle cooking. She was one of the 'food gurus' in the ground-breaking classic book on South Africa's top chefs, *Food Gurus Uncovered*.

Scott Webster Travelling and working extensively throughout Europe, North America and Asia, some call him 'the bright new wave' of Australian cuisine. He has a reputation for creating culinary masterpieces which highlight the quality of Australian produce.

Marvin Woods Beloved television host, lauded cookbook author and celebrated American chef. His infectious personality, signature bandanas and his wildly inventive take on food rooted in northern Africa, South America, the Caribbean and the Low Country all make him instantly recognisable.

Ingredients

4 (600g)	medium green tomatoes
1tsp (5ml)	salt
1ml	ground Peri-Peri
⅔ cup (190ml)	cornflour
2tbs (30ml)	all purpose flour
½ cup (125ml)	sunflower oil

Peri-Peri fried green tomatoes

Clayton Sherrod

Method

1. Slice tomatoes ½ centimetre thick.
2. Sprinkle with salt and ground Peri-Peri. Leave for 10 minutes.
3. Mix flour and cornflour well.
4. Coat tomato slices with cornflour mixture.
5. Heat oil over medium heat.
6. Fry tomatoes for 4 minutes per side until tender and golden brown.
7. Drain on paper towel.

Serves 4

Ingredients

2 cups (500g)	white sugar
1.5L	water
3 tbs (45ml)	lemon juice
½ cup (150ml)	whiskey
1 tbs (15ml)	sweet Peri-Peri, strained through a fine sieve
2	egg whites

Method

1. Boil water, sugar and lemon juice in a large pot for 5 minutes until sugar is dissolved.
2. Add lemon juice and sweet peri peri sauce.
3. Cool to room temperature.
4. Whisk egg whites to a soft peak and fold into syrup.
5. Churn in an ice cream machine until set.

Makes 1 litre sorbet

whiskey Peri-Peri sorbet

Arnold Tanzer

Ingredients

⅓ cup (60g)	button mushrooms, sliced
½ (80g)	onion, chopped
1 (80g)	green bell pepper, diced
1 cup (240g)	patna rice
2 cups (500ml)	fish stock (bouillon)
Pinch	saffron
Salt & pepper	to taste
⅔ cup (180g)	butter
12 (700g)	tiger prawns, cleaned (shells on)
3 tbs (45ml)	olive oil
1 tsp (5ml)	Peri-Peri oil
2 tbs (30g)	shallots, finely diced
½ cup (120ml)	fish sauce
¼ cup (60ml)	white wine
⅔ cup (180ml)	double (heavy) cream
1 tsp (5ml)	curry paste
⅔ cup (180ml)	béchamel sauce
1 (80g)	banana
1	sprig parsley – flat leafed
½ cup (60g)	almonds flakes, toasted
⅓ cup (60g)	sultanas
1 (1ml)	Peri-Peri, ground
¼ cup (60ml)	brandy

Mango salsa

½ (200g)	mango, peeled and diced
1 (100g)	tomato, peeled and diced
1 (1g)	Peri-Peri chilli

Method

1. Braise the onions, mushrooms and green bell pepper in half the butter for 2–3 minutes, then add rice.
2. Stir in fish stock, saffron and seasoning.
3. Cover and allow to cook for 20 minutes.
4. Add a knob of butter and stir in sultanas (keep warm).
5. Wash the prawns in running water and drain well.
6. Marinade in a little olive oil with chopped chilli and leave for 10 minutes.
7. Shallow fry the chopped shallot in butter until golden brown.
8. Add the prawns with the chilli and lightly cook for 2 minutes on each side.
9. Add brandy and flame.
10. Add the curry paste, white wine, white sauce and double cream. Bring to the boil.
11. Remove prawns and keep hot.
12. Reduce the liquid by half.
13. Add sliced bananas.
14. Return the prawns to the sauce. Adjust seasoning.
15. Add chopped flat-leafed parsley.
16. Serve with the saffron rice and sprinkle with toasted almonds.
17. Drizzle with a light chilli oil.
18. Mix mango, Peri-Peri chilli and tomato and serve as an accompaniment.

Serve 4-6

prawns maharani

Billy Gallagher

Ingredients

1 (± 1.5kg)	whole chicken
4tbs (60ml)	butter
1½ (375g)	onions, finely chopped
1 cup (375g)	celery, finely chopped
2 (375g)	green bell peppers, finely chopped
2 tsp (10ml)	Peri-Peri sauce- heat level of your preference
1 cup (300g)	Tasso – or smoked ham, finely chopped
1 cup (200ml)	tomato puree
2 cups (400g)	rice, uncooked- raw
3 cups (750ml)	chicken stock

Seasoning mix

2	whole bay leaves
1 tsp (5ml)	salt
1 tsp (5ml)	white pepper
1 tsp (5ml)	garlic powder
½ tsp (2ml)	coarse Peri-Peri flakes
¼ tsp (2ml)	black pepper

jambalaya

Paul Prudhomme

Method

1. Trim chicken carcass of all meat and skin (white and brown meat) and cut flesh into 2cm pieces.

2. Melt butter and add half of onion, celery and bell peppers to warm butter.

3. Add seasoning mix, Tasso (ham) and Peri-Peri sauce. Saute untill onions are dark brown (about 20 min) stirring constantly.

4. Add remaining vegetables and cook further 5 minutes.

5. Add tomato puree and simmer 5 minutes.

6. Add meat and simmer for 15 minutes. Add in rice and mix well. Reduce heat and simmer for about 12 minutes.

7. Add stock, bring to the boil . Reduce heat and simmer over very low heat until rice is tender but firm (about 15 minutes).

Serves 4 main or 8 starter portions.

Ingredients

24	oysters, fresh on the half shell
2 (240g)	tomatoes finely diced
2 (50g)	shallots finely chopped
2 (5ml)	Peri-Peri chilies seeded and finely diced
3 tbs (45ml)	coriander (cilantro) leaves
1 tbs (15ml)	extra virgin olive oil
Pinch	celery salt
To season	cracked black pepper

Peri-Peri oysters

Joanina Pastoll and Natalie Bell

Method

1. Remove the oysters from their shells. Use warm water to wash the shells, then pat dry. Place oysters back in their shells.

2. Mix tomato, shallots, Peri-Peri and coriander in a bowl.

3. Stir in lime juice and olive oil.

4. Season with celery salt and cracked black pepper.

5. Place a heaped teaspoon of the mixture on each oyster.

6. Slice extra lime wedges and serve.

Serves 4-6

Marinated salmon

1 (1kg)	side of salmon
½ cup (125ml)	sherry vinegar
2 cups (500g)	sea salt
1 cup (200g)	sugar
2 (30g)	limes, zested
½ cup (125ml)	lime juice
½ cup (30g)	coriander leaf, chopped
2 tbs (30g)	garlic, crushed

1. Dry the salmon side.
2. Combine all ingredients and spread over the salmon.
3. Let cure under weight for 6 hours, then clean off completely.
4. Slice and serve.

Roasted pineapple Peri-Peri dressing

2 (500g)	pineapple
2 (1g)	Peri-Peri chilli, cut in half, seeds removed
½ cup (30g)	coriander, chopped
½ cup (125ml)	fresh lime juice
¼ cup (60ml)	asian fish sauce
½ cup (125ml)	chives, chopped

1. Roast pineapple whole in skin wrapped in foil for approx 1 hour at 150°C to work the sugars which enhance the flavour.
2. Leave to cool and then peel and puree the flesh.
3. Add chilli, lime juice, fish sauce, coriander & season.

Plating

2	pomeloes, segmented
1	Peri-Peri chilli
30g	chives, sliced finely
¼ cup (30g)	red onion, finely diced
2 tbs (30ml)	olive oil
1	punnet mustard sprouts

1. Mix pomelo segments with chopped red Peri-Peri chilli, red onion, chives, olive oil and seasoning.
2. Evenly distribute onto 4 plates and top with 5 slices of salmon.
3. Spread dressing evenly and garnish with small mustard sprout bunches.
4. Grind a little pepper over and serve.

tasmanian salmon ceviche with roasted pineapple Peri-Peri dressing

Serves 4

Scott Webster

Ingredients

2 lbs (1kg)	prawns, peeled and deveined
¼ cup (60ml)	clarified butter
10 oz (300g)	shallots, chopped
4 (8g)	garlic cloves, crushed
1 tsp (2g)	coriander , ground
1 tsp (2g)	cumin ground
1 tsp (3g)	Peri-Peri, ground
2 cans (300g each)	artichoke hearts, drained, quartered
1 ½ cup (200g)	shitaki mushrooms, sliced
1 cup (250ml)	coconut milk
1 cup (250ml)	cream
¼ cup (60ml)	parmesan cheese, grated
3 tbs (45ml)	parsley, chopped
1 tsp (5ml)	salt
½ tsp (2.5ml)	black pepper

curry coconut prawns with artichokes & mushrooms

Clayton Sherrod

Method

1. Sauté prawns, shallots and garlic in butter over medium heat.

2. Add coriander, cumin and Peri-Peri and fry for a further 1 minute.

3. Add artichokes and mushrooms and cook on low heat briefly.

4. Add coconut milk, cream, parmesan cheese, parsley, salt and black pepper. Simmer for 5 minutes and serve with steamed rice.

Serves 6

Ingredients

500g	beef fillet, sliced into very thin slices
1 (500g)	large farmstyle round sourdough bread
1 (150g)	small brinjal
2 (300g)	medium avocados
¼ cup (60ml)	olive oil
3 tbs (45ml)	garlic, crushed
1 (150g)	red bell pepper
125ml	Peri-Peri sauce

picnic bread with layers of grilled brinjal, avocado & Peri-Peri beef fillet

Rochelle Shaetzl

Method

1. Marinade meat in the Peri-Peri sauce.

2. Cut the top of the bread and hollow the inside out. Leave a 1½ cm wall.

3. Slice the brinjal into thin slices, and layer on a flat baking sheet.

4. Deseed the bell pepper and cut into segments. Place next to the brinjal on the baking sheet.

5. Drizzle with the olive oil and garlic and roast under a grill until slightly charred. Remove from heat.

6. Panfry the marinated meat quickly (1 minute on each side).

7. Layer the inside of the bread with the roasted bell pepper. Season.

8. Place a layer of grilled brinjal on the roasted bell pepper.

9. Layer the grilled meat on the grilled brinjal.

10. Slice the avocado into slivers and layer on top of the meat. Pour the pan juices over the avocado.

11. Press all the layers down firmly and replace the 'lid of the bread'.

12. Slice into 5cm chunks and serve with a green salad.

Serves 4-6

Ingredients

3 tbs (45ml)	sunflower oil
10 (50g)	shallots, peeled and finely sliced
4 (20g)	garlic cloves, pounded
1tbs (15ml)	preserved soybeans, washed, drained and pounded
1 ½ lbs (700g)	pork foreleg (skin-on), cut into chunks
1 tsp (5ml)	cinnamon, ground
2tbs (30ml)	dark soy sauce
6 cups (1.5l)	water
2	sugarcanes (about 8-cm lengths), peeled
1 tsp (5ml)	salt
1 tsp (5ml)	white sugar
1 can (410g)	bamboo shoots, canned, blanched and cut into chunks
2 (7g)	Peri-Peri chillies

asian-style braised pork

Peter Knipp

Method

1. Heat sunflower oil in a wok and stir-fry the sliced shallots until lightly browned.
2. Add in pounded garlic and preserved soybeans. Stir-fry for another 2 minutes until fragrant.
3. Add pork and cinnamon and stir for a few more minutes.
4. Add soy sauce and water and simmer for 10 minutes.
5. Add sugarcanes, salt and sugar and simmer until pork is tender.

To serve: Place the blanched bamboo shoots into a serving dish and ladle the braised pork over and garnish with torn chillies. Serves 4.

Ingredients
Soufflé

200ml	béchamel
¼ cup (40g)	goat's cheese, creamed or pureed
6	egg whites
½ tsp (2ml)	salt
2½ tbs	lemon juice
¼ cup (40g)	goat's cheese, for lining the ramekins
1 tbs (15m)	unsalted butter, creamed
¼ cup (50g)	dried white bread crumbs, no crust
1 tbs (15ml)	Peri-Peri powder, ground

Vinaigrette

1 tbs (15ml)	hazelnut oil
3tbs (45ml)	sunflower oil
15ml (1tbs)	white wine vinegar
2g	basil, torn
2g	fresh thyme leaves
½ tsp (2ml)	salt & pepper

soufflé of goat's cheese and Peri-Peri with a hazelnut and herb salad

Stefano Strafella

Method
Soufflé

1. Preheat oven to 170°C.
2. Prepare a basic béchamel sauce with butter, milk and flour. Once cooked remove the sauce from heat and stir in the egg yolks and goat's cheese and then set aside.
3. In a large bowl beat the egg whites to light peaks with the salt, add the lemon juice and continue to beat until the mixture is smooth and stiff.
4. Beat ⅕ of the egg white mixture into the base mixture until it is loose.
5. Add the rest of the egg white mixture into the base and fold in gently. Set aside.
6. Blend the crumbs and Peri-Peri together until fine.
7. Butter the ramekins, then layer with the crumbed mixture.
8. Half fill the ramekins with the soufflé mixture and add some diced cheese into the middle.
9. Top up with more soufflé mixture and smooth off with a spatula.
10. Wipe inside edge of the ramekins to prevent soufflé spilling over.
11. Place the ramekins in a shallow roasting tin, pour in some warm water (up to ⅔ height of ramekins) and bake in a preheated oven at 170°C for 18 minutes.
12. If twice baking remove soufflés from ramekins and store on an oiled tray until ready to serve.
13. Return to the oven for 5 minutes or until slightly crisp.

Vinaigrette

Combine all ingredients together and mix well.

Serves 4–6

Ingredients

2tbs (30ml)	light olive oil	¼ cup (60m)	fresh orange juice
2 (300g)	red bell peppers, diced	2 tbs (30ml)	soft brown sugar
2 (300g)	yellow bell peppers, diced	2 tbs (30ml)	fresh lemon juice
½ (80g)	red onion, finely diced	2 tbs (30ml)	extra virgin olive oil
2 (50g)	scallions, roughly chopped	1 tbs (15ml)	pickling spices, ground
¼ (80g)	cucumber, seeded and diced	½ (1ml)	Peri-Peri chilli
		¼ cup (60ml)	flat leaf parsley, finely chopped
¼ cup (60ml)	champagne vinegar		
¼ cup (60ml)	white balsamic vinegar	2 lbs (1kg)	fresh jumbo lump crab

Peri-Peri jumbo lump crab escabeche

Marvin Woods

Method

1. Place light olive oil in a medium sauté pan over medium heat.

2. Add peppers, onions and Peri-Peri and sauté for 2 to 3 minutes.

3. Remove from heat and allow to cool.

4. Once vegetables have cooled, place them in a medium-sized bowl.

5. Add scallions and cucumber.

6. In another medium-sized bowl, place the vinegar, orange juice, lemon juice and brown sugar. Blend until sugar dissolves. Whisk in the olive oil.

7. Season to taste. Add crab. Pour in vegetables. Gently mix together.

8. Refrigerate and marinade for up to 2 hours.

9. Serve cold as a starter.

Serves 6

Ingredients

500g	fresh salmon fillet, finely chopped
½ cup (100g)	onions, finely chopped
1 (120g)	green bell pepper, seeded and diced
2	large eggs, slightly beaten
¼ tsp (1.25ml)	Peri-Peri, ground
½ cup (125m)l	all-purpose flour
½ tbs (7.5ml)	salt
¼ tsp (1.25ml)	garlic powder
½ cup (100g)	all purpose flour
1	egg
¼ cup	cornmeal
½ cup (125ml)	vegetable oil for cooking

salmon croquettes

Wilbert Jones

Method

1. Combine salmon, onion, bell pepper, eggs, Peri-Peri, flour, salt and garlic in a bowl and mix well.

2. Divide the mixture into 8 equal portions. Shape each portion into a croquette shape.

3. Dip each one in flour, egg and then in cornmeal and set aside.

4. Heat the vegetable oil in a large heavy pan over medium until hot.

5. Cook the croquettes about 4 to 5 minutes on each side or until they are firm in the centre and have turned golden brown all around.

6. Drain on paper towel and keep warm till ready to serve. Serve with a green salad.

Serves 4

Ingredients

½ cup (120g)	butter
½ cup (125ml)	brown sugar
½ cup (125ml)	white sugar
1 (90g)	lemon, sliced
½ tsp (2.5ml)	vanilla extract
3-4 (400g)	bananas, sliced
¼ cup (60ml)	dark rum
6 cups (1.5l)	vanilla ice-cream
2g	Peri-Peri flakes

bananas foster

Clayton Sherrod

Method

1. Heat butter, brown sugar, granulated sugar, sliced lemon and vanilla extract in a pan until hot and bubbly.

2. Add bananas.

3. Remove from heat. Add dark rum, return to heat and light to burn alcohol off.

4. Scoop ice-cream into individual serving bowls and spoon banana mixture over ice-cream.

5. Sprinkle with dried Peri-Peri chilli.

Serves 6

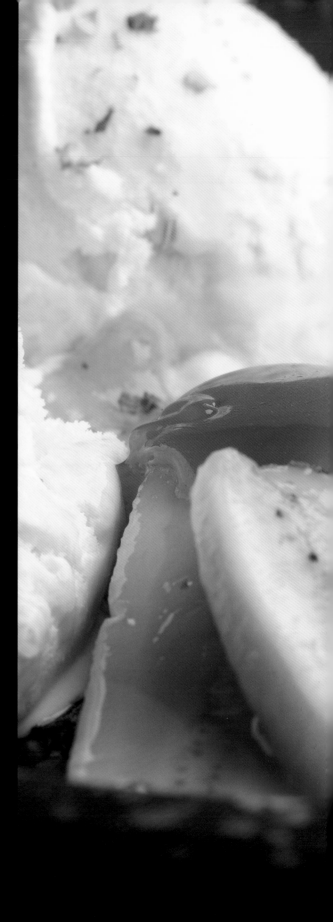

Ingredients

1 tbs (15ml)	sunflower oil
¼ cup (50g)	leeks, finely diced
1lb (500g)	minced pork
2 (60g)	white bread slices
¼ cup (60ml)	milk
3 cloves (15g)	garlic, crushed
Pinch	nutmeg
3 (6g)	Peri-Peri chillies, chopped
2 tbs (15ml)	coriander
2 tbs (15ml)	ginger, crushed
1 (60g)	egg
Pinch	paprika

malton meatballs

Brian Turner

Tomato sauce

½ cup (125g)	butter
1 (10g)	shallot, finely diced
1 (5g)	garlic clove, crushed
1 (2g)	chilli, minced
1 cup (250ml)	dry white wine
1tbs (15ml)	Worcestershire sauce
1 tsp (5ml)	celery salt
1 can (410g)	tomatoes, chopped
6 (900g)	tomatoes, skinned, seeded

Method

1. Heat oil and gently fry the leeks, garlic and Peri-Peri for 2-3 minutes, take off and cool.
2. Add milk to the bread and soak, squeeze out and add to pork, with the leek and garlic, coriander and ginger.
3. Season and add enough beaten egg to make into a mouldable mix.
4. Mould and fry in frying pan to colour quickly on the outside. Put into tomato sauce and cook out for 10 minutes.

Tomato sauce

1. Melt butter in a frying pan. Add shallot, garlic and chilli, saute for 2-3 minutes.
2. Add white wine and reduce by ⅔.
3. Add Worcestershire sauce and celery salt and stir.
4. Add tomatoes and simmer for 5 minutes.
5. Add meatballs and simmer for further 5 minutes.
6. Add oregano and chopped tomatoes.
7. Simmer for a further 5 minutes and serve.

Serves 4

steamed lemon puddings with chilli bitter chocolate sauce

Paul Hartman

Ingredients

2/5 cup (100ml)	lemon curd
½ cup (110g)	self raising flour, sifted three times
½ cup (110g)	butter
½ cup (110g)	castor sugar
3	eggs
¼ cup (25g)	zest of 2 lemons

Bitter chocolate sauce

¼ cup (50ml)	sweet Peri-Peri sauce, strained
1 cup (250ml)	cream
1 cup (250g)	bitter chocolate

Method

Lemon puddings

1. Pre-heat oven to 180°C
2. Butter 6 ramekins dish well and spread lemon curd at the bottom of each.
3. Beat butter and sugar till fluffy. Add eggs one at a time and continue to beat.
4. Fold in flour. Stir in lemon zest.
5. Pour mixture into ramekin dishes on top of curd.
6. Cover with parchment and then with muslin cloth.
7. Tie down the muslin and then place in an 180°C oven in a water bath.
8. Bake for 45 minutes.

Bitter chocolate sauce

1. Heat cream till boiling point.
2. Add the sweet Peri-Peri sauce and chocolate.
3. Remove from heat and stir till chocolate has dissolved.

Enjoy warm with crème fraiche. Serves 4.

Ingredients

4 × 150g	cod fish or kingklip fillets
400ml	olive oil
350g	straw potato chips
4	eggs
4	egg yolks
10g	parsley, finely chopped
350g	onion, sliced
4	cloves garlic
2	bay leaves
50ml	olive oil
200g	green asparagus
100g	baby green asparagus, blanched

Garlic chips

100g	garlic, peeled and sliced
250ml	milk

Herb oil

100g	variety fresh herbs (basil, chives, dill, parsley)
80ml	olive oil (extra virgin)
20g dry	Peri-Peri flakes

*á brás of green asparagus
with olive oil, poached cod
and Peri-Peri flakes*

Fausti Arnoldi

Method

1. Peel big green asparagus and cut off fibrous ends.
2. Cook in salty boiling water until cooked but still al dente, plunge in iced water immediately.
3. Remove from the water, dry and cut diagonally and refrigerate.
4. Warm the 400ml of olive oil to 80°C.
5. Place the fish in a tray that just fits the fish, pour the hot olive oil over it and place in a hot oven for 8 to 10 minutes.
6. Once the fish begins to free some milky liquid that stays suspended in olive oil, it is ready.
7. Make the cebolada by heating the olive oil, onions and garlic until they begin to colour, season well with salt and pepper.
8. For serving add the cut asparagus to this cebolada,
9. Add the potato chips.
10. Put the eggs and yolks thru a sieve and add at the end.
11. Stir well and add parsley, season to taste.
12. Do not over cook the mixture should be served very moist.

Garlic chips

1. Cook garlic in milk for 2 minutes and repeat this process 3 times using fresh milk each time.
2. Drain and dry garlic slices.
3. Fry in peanut oil until golden, place on absorbent paper and keep in a dry place.

Herb oil

1. Pick leaves and discard stalk from herbs.
2. Wash and dry the herbs well.
3. Chop finely with a knife and place in a liquidizer with olive oil, blend for 10 minutes.
4. Let it rest in a cool area for 12 hours, strain through a fine sieve.

You should have a nice green aromatic oil.
Keep refrigerated for a maximum 15 days.

Plating

1. Place the á bras at middle of the plate
2. Place poached fish on top with the baby asparagus
3. Sprinkle the cod with Peri-Peri flakes and garnish with garlic chips.
4. Drop herb oil around and serve.

Serves 4

Custard and broth

2 (300g)	onions, finely chopped
2 (10g)	garlic cloves, crushed
1 tbs (15ml)	ginger, grated
2 tbs (30ml)	olive oil
1kg	sweetcorn
2 cans (600ml)	coconut cream
3	eggs
To taste	salt & pepper
60ml	Peri-Peri sauce

Salad

½ cup (100g)	sweetcorn
½ cup (100g)	butter
6 (50g)	spring onion, sliced thinly at an angle
1 (80g)	red onion, chopped finely
1 (100g)	red pepper, small brunoise
3 (50g)	radishes, jullienne
½ (80g)	cucumber, brunoise
2 tbs (30ml)	parsley, chopped
½ cup (100ml)	olive oil
To taste	salt & pepper
2 tbs (30ml)	Peri-Peri sauce
1 tbs (5g)	chervil

Peri-Peri sweetcorn custard with a toasted sweetcorn salad

Jodi-Ann Palmer

Custard and broth

1. Grease the dariole moulds well. Fill a bain marie with 1cm of water.
2. Saute onion, garlic and ginger in a little olive oil until completely soft. Add sweetcorn and coconut cream and bring to a gentle simmer. Allow to simmer until the sweetcorn is completely soft.
3. Blend the simmered mixture until smooth then pass it through a sieve.
4. Measure out 2 cups (500ml) of this mixture into a mixing bowl and set the rest aside.
5. Add the eggs to the 500ml mixture in the mixing bowl. Add Peri-Peri sauce and season well. Blend well and pass again through a sieve.
6. Pour the mixture into the small moulds and place in the bain marie.
7. Bake at 150°C until just set. Allow to cool, then turn out of moulds.
8. Season the sweetcorn mixture in the saucepan well (add more coconut milk if necessary). Use a blender to foam it a little.

Salad

1. Toast the salad sweetcorn in the butter until just golden.
2. Toss all the salad ingredients with the sweetcorn and season well – set aside.

To plate

Place each custard on a plate, pour some of the broth around it and spoon a few tablespoons of salad at an angle across it. Drizzle with a little olive oil and serve. Garnish with chervil if available.

Serves 6.

Ingredients

1lb (500g)	baby calamari tubes	**Salad**		
3 tbs (45ml)	olive oil	2 cups (150g)	salad greens
1 tsp (5ml)	salt	1 (200g)	pineapple
1 tsp (5ml)	cracked black pepper		peeled and cubed
1 (30ml)	lemon, juiced	½ cup (100g)	cashews, toasted
3 tbs (45ml)	soya sauce	1 (150g)	red pepper, jullienne
1 tsp (5ml)	ginger, grated	½ cup (125ml)	olive oil
1 tsp (5ml)	garlic, crushed	2 tbs (30ml)	raspberry vinegar
2-3 (5ml)	Peri-Peri finely chopped	To taste	salt and pepper

Peri-Peri fried calamari with pineapple and cashew nut salad

Vanie Padayachee

Method

1. Heat olive oil in a heavy-bottom sauce pan.

2. Sauté calamari for 3 to 5 minutes.

3. Add the rest of the ingredients and saute for a further 5 minutes, turning the calamari to cook evenly.

4. Remove from heat and set aside until required.

5. Mix all salad ingredients together.

6. Place the salad in the off centre of the plate.

7. Place the calamari in front of the salad and drizzle over with the sauce of the calamari. Serve warm.

Serves 4

Ingredients

Koeksisters

1 cup (240g)	all purpose flour
¼ tsp (1,25ml)	salt
1 tbs (15ml)	baking powder
1 tsp (5ml)	butter
1	egg
¼ cup (60ml)	milk
sunflower oil for deep frying	

Ginger and Peri Peri syrup

3 cups (800g)	sugar
1½ cup (375ml)	water
1 tbs (10ml)	ginger, freshly grated
½ tsp (2.5ml)	crème of tartar
½ tsp (2.5ml)	Peri-Peri chilli, coarse
½ tsp (2.5ml)	Peri-Peri sauce

malay koeksisters with Peri-Peri and ginger

Garth Stroebel

Method

1. Place all the dry ingredients in the bowl. Add the wet ingredients and enough milk to form a soft dough. Refrigerate overnight to rest the dough.

2. Prepare syrup by boiling all syrup ingredients together till sugar has dissolved and syrup has a smooth shiny appearance. Place syrup in freezer to cool down quickly to 2°C. (Do not freeze).

3. Roll out the dough to 1cm thick. Cut into rectangles of 6cm x3cm. Make 2x5cm cuts 1cm from each other from the one side of the rectangle to the other side, but do not cut through, so the 3 strips are still attached at the top end. Plait from top end down and pinch bottom ends together.

4. Heat sunflower oil in a deep saucepan till 90°C.

5. Deep fry each koeksister till golden. (turn in oil , to achieve even colour)

6. Remove from oil and immediately submerse into ice cold syrup, whilst still hot. Do not allow to drain before dipping in syrup- otherwise koeksisters won't absorb cold syrup.

7. Leave to soak.

8. Drain out after 5 minutes and serve.

Makes 24 koeksisters

Ingredients

1 (1.2kg)	medium rabbit, portioned
12 (600g)	pickling onions
15 (1kg)	new potatoes
¼ cup (60ml)	port wine
1 tbs (10g)	parsley, chopped
for frying	sunflower oil

Marinade

6 (12g)	garlic cloves, crushed
1	bay leaf
1 cup (250ml)	white wine
1tbs (15ml)	white vinegar
¼ cup (60ml)	Peri-Peri sauce
1tbs (2g)	thyme, fresh
½ cup (100m)	lard
1 cup (125g)	presunto (smoked ham)

braised rabbit

Mimi Jardim

Method

1. Mix marinade ingredients together, add rabbit portions and marinade overnight.
2. Remove rabbit from the marinade and keep the marinade aside.
3. Pre-heat oven to 160°C.
4. Melt the lard in a pan and brown rabbit pieces.
5. Place browned rabbit pieces in a casserole dish with a lid, pour leftover marinade over the rabbit and cover the dish.
6. Bake in pre-heated oven for approx 60 minutes or until the meat is completely tender.
7. Parboil potatoes and then deep-fry till golden.
8. 10 minutes before removing the rabbit from the oven, place the potatoes and port wine into the casserole dish and stir them in.
9. Remove from the oven, season well with salt, pepper and parsley.

Serve 6

Peri-Peri paste

Ingredients

1 cup (300g)	Peri-Peri chillies
½ cup (100g)	fresh ginger, peeled
12 (25g)	garlic cloves
1 (150g)	onion
⅘ cup (200ml)	vegetable oil
½ cup (50g)	cilantro leaf, chopped
1 (100g)	lemon, cut in half

Method

1. In a blender, put all ingredients except the lemon juice and blend until you have a fine paste.
2. Place in small containers and freeze till required.

grilled baby chicken with Peri-Peri and lemon atchar

Coco Fathi

Ingredients

2 (1.5kg)	baby chickens (700g each)
3 tbs (50g)	Peri-Peri paste - see above
¼ cup (70g)	lemon atchar (10 slices)
2 (300g)	onions
½ cup (100g)	ginger, peeled & sliced
½ cup (100g)	coriander, chopped
To taste	salt and pepper

Method

1. Lift the skin of the baby chickens and insert 25g of Peri-Peri, 5 slices of lemon atchar per baby chicken with 50g sliced ginger.
2. Stuff the inside with a paste made of the rest of the Peri-Peri, chopped onions, lemon atchar and coriander.
3. Cover the baby chicken in a bowl and refrigerate overnight.
4. Butterfly the baby chickens and brush all over with the stuffing. Season to taste.
5. Grill the chicken on a low open flame to allow for smoke infusion. Turn often.

Serves 4

Ingredients

1 (40g)	small block tamarind		3	cloves
1 cup (250ml)	water, boiling		2	bay leaves
3 (450g)	onions, sliced		1kg	lamb chops
2 tbs (25ml)	vegetable oil		2 tbs (35ml)	nutmeg, grated
5 (10g)	garlic cloves, sliced		2 tbs (30ml)	black pepper, freshly ground
½ tsp (2.5ml)	Peri-Peri, ground		3 tbs (45ml)	brown sugar
5	allspice berries		To taste salt	

denningvleis

Cass Abrahams

Method

1. Soak the tamarind in boiling water, then strain to remove seeds.

2. Spread all the onions on the base of a saucepan.

3. Sprinkle the oil, garlic, Peri-Peri, allspice, cloves and bay leaves over the onions.

4. Layer the lamb chops on top of the onions and pour over the tamarind sauce so meat is covered.

5. Sprinkle over the nutmeg, black pepper, salt and sugar.

6. Close with a tight fitting lid and cook on a high heat for 15 minutes, then reduce the heat and simmer for a further 45 minutes.

7. Do not allow the dish to dry out and add extra water if necessary. The consistency should be thick and sticky. Season and serve with rice.

Serves 6

Ingredients

1 (1kg)	whole line fish, cleaned	300g	okra sliced thinly
5 (150g)	fresh limes	1kg	wild spinach, washed
½ cup (125ml)	olive oil	2 (350g)	onions sliced
¼ cup (60ml)	Peri-Peri sauce	6 (900g)	tomatoes diced
2 tbs (30ml)	lemon juice	15g	Peri-Peri seasoning
1kg	yams, peeled and cubed	100ml	Peri-Peri sauce
500ml	milk	40ml	olive oil
1 cup (200g)	butter	15g	butter
		50g	melon seeds toasted

grilled line fish with yam mash

Citrum Kumalo

Method

1. Blend olive oil, Peri-Peri sauce and lemon juice to smooth consistency.

2. Cut open the fish skin, squeeze lime juice over it and spread the Peri-Peri paste over that.

3. Turn fish, squeeze limes and spread remainder of paste over skin side.

4. Cook yams covered in water with a pinch of salt until soft and water has almost evaporated. Then mash. Add butter and milk and continue cooking until butter and milk is well combined. Season and set aside.

5. In a separate pan sauté onions, add okra and simmer for 2 minutes. Add tomatoes and cook for about 5 minutes.

6. Add spinach to the okra mixture. Add Peri-Peri seasoning. Steam for 2 minutes.

7. Plate a generous portion of mash in centre of plate. Place a portion of fish on top of yam mash. Top with spinach & okra stew and garnish with toasted melon seeds.

Serves 4-6

Ingredients

6 large (600g)	green bananas or plantains, with skin on
2 cups (500ml)	vegetable or groundnut oil for frying

For the filling

2 tbs (30ml)	coriander leaves, chopped
2 tbs (30ml)	fresh ginger, grated
3tbs (45ml)	seedless raisins
2	green chillies, deseeded and finely chopped
1 tbs (15ml)	roasted cumin seeds
2 tsp (10ml)	salt

For the sauce

2 cups(500ml)	natural yoghurt
1 tsp (5ml)	fennel seeds, roasted and ground
1 tsp (5ml)	ground coriander seeds, roasted
¼ (1.25ml)	Peri-Peri, ground
2 tbs (30ml)	cream

Garnish

1 tbs (15ml)	roasted desiccated coconut
1 tbs (15ml)	pomegranate seeds
5g	fresh coriander leaves, chopped

stuffed plantain dumplings soaked in yoghurt

Reza Muhammad

Method

1. Cut the plantains into thirds or quarters depending on their size, leaving the skin on.
2. Bring a pan of water to the boil, add the plantain slices and cook until tender. Drain and allow to cool. Peel and mash the plantains.
3. In a separate bowl combine all the filling ingredients.
4. Oil hands liberally and lightly press one tablespoon of the mashed plantain into the palm of one hand. Make a well in the centre and add a generous pinch of the filling mixture.
5. Close the plantain mixture over the stuffing and very lightly roll into a ball. Continue with the remaining mixture until used up.
6. Heat the oil in a frying pan or wok over a medium heat and add the plantain dumplings. Fry until crisp and golden, then remove and drain on kitchen paper.
7. Make the sauce in separate bowl. Mix the yoghurt with the spices and salt to taste. Add a little cream to the mixture until it has the consistency of double cream.
8. Pour half of the sauce onto an oval dish with sides. Place the dumplings on top and then cover the dumplings with the rest of the yoghurt mixture.
9. Garnish with the toasted coconut, pomegranate and the chopped coriander.

Serves 4-6

Butternut soup

¼ cup (40g)	butter
4 cups (1kg)	butternut, peeled and diced
1 tsp (3g)	Peri-Peri, coarse
1 (150g)	onion, diced
½ tsp (3ml)	turmeric
10	curry leaves
½	star anise
1 inch (2cm)	cinnamon stick
2 tbs (30ml)	honey
10 oz (300ml)	milk
10 oz (300m)	vegetable stock
3 oz (100ml)	cream

1. Melt butter in a large saucepan.
2. Add butternut, Peri-Peri, onion, turmeric, curry leaves, star anise and cinnamon stick and sauté until softened.
3. Add honey, milk and vegetable stock and bring to the boil. Reduce heat, simmer until butternut begins to disintegrate - about 20 minutes.
4. Remove cinnamon, anise and curry leaves.
5. Using a hand-held stab mixer, blend to smooth consistency.
6. Pass through a fine strainer into a clean saucepan and reheat. Add cream and adjust the seasoning. Keep warm.

Prawns

4	prawns, peeled and deveined
1	egg, beaten
3 tbs (50g)	all purpose flour
½ tsp (3ml)	garam masala
¼ cup (50g)	fine beaten rice
1 cup (250ml)	canola oil for frying

1. Heat the oil in a small saucepan.
2. Combine the flour and masala.
3. Coat the prawns in the flour mixture and shake off any excess. Then dip the prawns into egg and coat with the fine beaten rice.
4. Fry until golden and done (3 minutes).
5. Drain on kitchen paper and keep warm.

Garlic foam

1	bay leaf
2	gelatine leaves, soaked in cold water
1	egg white
150ml	milk
3	garlic cloves, peeled and chopped

1. Heat milk, garlic and bay leaf in a small saucepan to scald.
2. Drain the gelatine and place in a tall container with the egg white.
3. Strain the hot milk onto the gelatine and egg white.
4. Using a hand-held stab mixer, process until foam is visible on the surface.
5. Remove the stab mixer and spoon the foam onto the soup.

Serves 4

Peri-Peri butternut and winter squash soup with deep-fried prawns

Garth Stroebel

Filling

3 tbs (50g)	laksa paste
2 (2g)	Peri-Peri chillies, finely chopped
2 cups (500g)	portabello mushrooms, thinly sliced
1 med (180g)	onion, finely chopped
1 tsp (5ml)	ginger, grated
1 tsp (5ml)	garlic, crushed
2 tsp (10ml)	salt
1 tsp (5ml)	black pepper
1 tsp (5ml)	mint, finely chopped
3 tbs (45ml)	olive oil
3 tbs (45ml)	butter

Spring rolls

10 sheets	spring roll pastry cut in triangle shape
1	egg white
½ cup (100g)	cornflour

Preserved lemon and coriander salsa

1 med (60g)	inside of preserved lemon removed and diced small
¼ (50g)	red peppers diced small
1	small green chilli, finely chopped
1 tsp (5ml)	coriander, finely chopped
1 tsp (5ml)	red wine vinegar
½ tsp (2.5ml)	black pepper

spicy laksa and portabella spring rolls with preserved chilli lemon and coriander salsa

Vanie Padayachee

Method
Spring roll filling
1. Heat oil and butter heavy bottom sauce pan.
2. Add in the rest of the ingredients and sauté for 5 minutes
3. Remove from heat and cool down.

Spring rolls
1. Dust work surface with cornflour
2. Place spring roll pastry onto surface with the point away from you
3. Place mushroom mixture into centre of pastry
4. Brush the end of the pastry with egg white
5. Roll the pastry to form a cigar. Tuck in the end properly or the mixture will ooze out.
6. Deep fry spring rolls and set onto kitchen towel to drain excess oil. Set aside until required

Preserved lemon and coriander salsa
Place all ingredients into a bowel and mix well

Serve 4-6

Basic pasta recipe

3	whole eggs
1½ cup (300g)	all purpose flour
	olive oil

1. Combine all the ingredients in a food processor - should look like coarse meal. Remove and knead. The dough can also be hand mixed.
2. Pasta dough should be smooth, elastic and just slightly moist.
3. Cover dough and rest.

Filling

1	cup (200g) cooked spinach (all water drained)
¼ cup (30g)	parmesan cheese, grated
½ cup(120g)	Boursin cheese
¼ cup (60g)	pine nuts, toasted
Pinch	grated nutmeg
3 tbs (5g)	parsley, chopped
2-3	whole Peri-Peri chillies
1 (180g)	onion, finely chopped
1 tbs (2g)	black pepper, crushed
3tbs (50g)	butter
⅔ cup (100ml)	cream
1	egg, slightly beaten

1. Sauté onion with garlic. Add chopped chilli.
2. Make sure that the onions are cooked thoroughly.
3. Add cream and reduce by half and blend with a stab mixer.
4. Add chopped spinach and cook. Blend again if needed.
5. Incorporate both cheeses. Add parsley. Season to taste.
6. Cool before use.

Tortellini

1. Roll out pasta dough into long thin rectangles.
2. Cut out circles, 5cm in diameter with a round cookie cutter.
3. Place ¼ teaspoon of filling into the centre of each round.
4. Brush egg on the bottom half of the round and fold over to seal. Fold back around your finger and turn down the edge to form a tortellini.

spinach boursin tortellini with Peri-Peri

Rudi Liebenberg

Rustic tomato and chorizo sauce

⅖ cup (100ml)	olive oil
4 tsp (20ml)	chilli oil
4 (5g)	Peri-Peri chillies
2 (10ml)	garlic cloves
150g	chorizo, sliced
8	strands saffron
½ cup (150g)	peas
⅘ cup (200g)	slow roasted tomatoes
4 (80g)	spring onions sliced
8	basil leaves
10g	Italian parsley

1. Heat up olive oil and chilli oil
2. Add all garlic and Peri-Peri chilli.
3. Add chorizo slices and saffron.
4. Add peas, tomatoes and spring onions.
5. Chop basil and parsley and add.
6. Simmer for 2 minutes.
7. Add sauce to pasta and stir through.
8. Serve with parmesan shavings on top.

Green chilli and coriander pesto

4 (20ml)	cloves garlic
8	small bunches fresh coriander
6	small green chillies
Pinch	course salt
30g	pine nuts, toasted
120g	parmesan cheese, grated
100ml	olive oil

1. In a food processor blend garlic and basil.
2. Add pine nuts, continue blending.
3. Gradually add the cheese. Blend.
4. When smooth add olive oil.

Serves 4

Tempura batter

½ cup (125ml)	tempura flour
1 cup (250ml)	chilled soda water
3 tbs (45ml)	Peri-Peri spice or to taste
½ tsp (2.5ml)	salt
3	strips fresh snoek, deboned
16-20	prawns cleaned, heads on

1. Mix the flour, salt and spice together in a mixing bowl.
2. Add the soda water slowly while constantly whisking. The batter should cover the back of a spoon.
3. Dip snoek and prawns in batter mix. Allow excess batter to drip off.
4. Fry until golden in 180°C oil. Drain and season.

Salad

20g	crispy red and green lettuce
1 (20g)	spring onion thinly sliced
½ small (80g)	red onion thinly julienne
1 (15g)	red radish thinly sliced
3 tbs (45ml)	olive oil

1. Combine the salad leaves and onion in a salad bowl and toss with the olive oil.
2. Add the radish just before serving.

Mayonnaise

3 tbs (45ml)	Peri-Peri sauce
1 cup (25cm)	mayonnaise

1. Add the Peri-Peri sauce to the mayonnaise and blend evenly.

Garnish

1	green banana
15ml	smoked paprika
2g	onion sprouts

1. Slice the bananas as thinly as possible.
2. Fry until golden in 180°C oil. Drain and season with the paprika and salt.

Serves 1

Peri-Peri snoek and prawn tempura with crispy salad and Peri-Peri mayonnaise

Reuben Riffel

Ingredients
Pastry

2 cups (420g)	all-purpose flour
½ cup (120g)	white sugar
1 tsp (5m)	salt
1 cup (250g)	butter, cut into 24 pieces
3-5 tbs (45-75ml)	cold water

Filling

5 (5g)	Peri-Peri chillies, dried
2 ½ cups (500g)	Smytha figs, dried, stemmed and coarsely cut
2 cup (500ml)	white wine
⅔ cup (150g)	sugar
2tbs (20g)	unsalted butter
¼ cup (60ml)	whiskey
1tbs (15ml)	vanilla extract
1 cup (200g)	walnuts, coarsely broken
½ tsp (2ml)	cayenne pepper
	Crème fraîche

walnut and smytha fig tart with Peri-Peri chillies

Topsy Venter

Method

Pastry

1. Place the flour, sugar and salt in a bowl, mix well.

2. Add butter and, with your fingers, combine just until the mixture resembles coarse meal.

3. Add water and form into a ball. Wrap in plastic and refrigerate for 2 hours or up to 2 days.

4. Pre-heat oven to 190°C. Remove pastry from fridge.

6. Press the pastry into a 25cm tart pan to make an oven bottom layer, press up the sides and extend a small ridge above the top edge of pan tart.

7. Cover with foil, fill with pie weights or dried beans. Blind bake 20 minutes.

8. Remove paper, cover only the edges and bake for 10 to 15 minutes more until the crust is light brown.

9. Remove from oven and let cool to room temperature before filling.

Filling

1. Cover the chillies with boiling water and let soak for 2-3 hours until soft and pliable. Remove seeds and stem, then finely chop and set aside.

2. Bring the figs, wine and sugar to boill in heavy-bottomed saucepan.

3. Reduce the heat and cook for 10-15 minutes until the figs are tender and the liquid syrupy.

4. Add the butter, whiskey, vanilla extract, walnuts, cayenne pepper and reserved chillies; mix well until the butter is melted. Remove from heat and cool slightly.

5. Fill the tart shell and serve; optionally with a drizzle of crème fraîche.

Serves 6-8

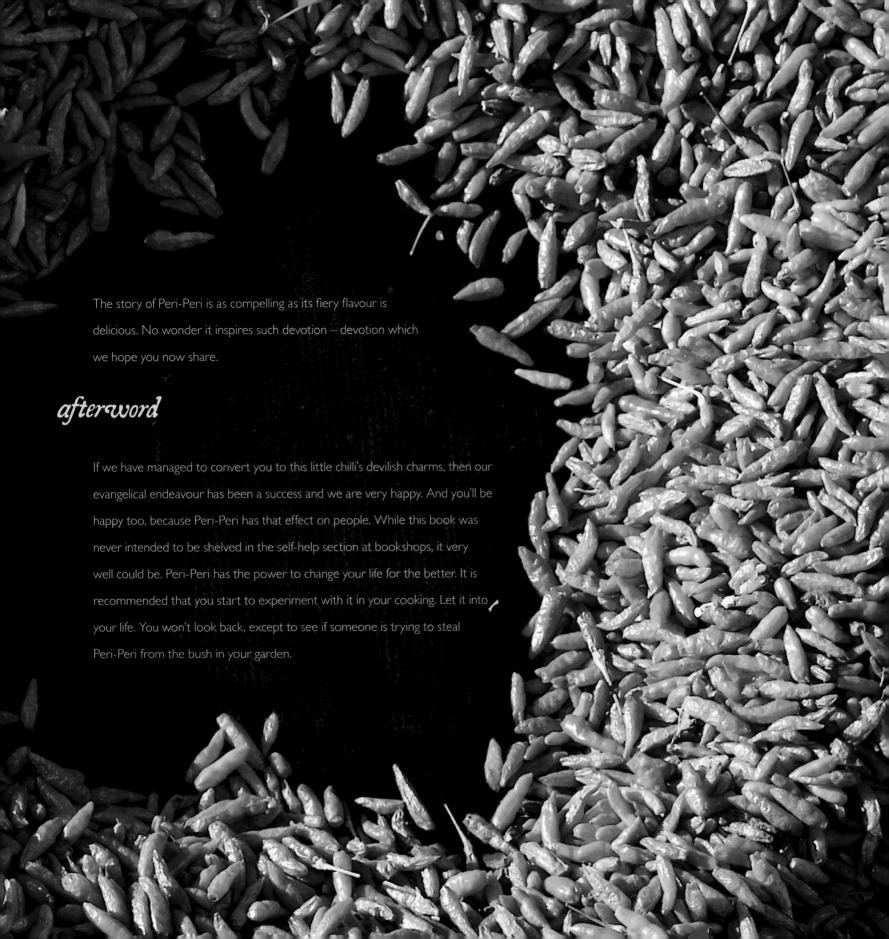

The story of Peri-Peri is as compelling as its fiery flavour is delicious. No wonder it inspires such devotion – devotion which we hope you now share.

afterword

If we have managed to convert you to this little chilli's devilish charms, then our evangelical endeavour has been a success and we are very happy. And you'll be happy too, because Peri-Peri has that effect on people. While this book was never intended to be shelved in the self-help section at bookshops, it very well could be. Peri-Peri has the power to change your life for the better. It is recommended that you start to experiment with it in your cooking. Let it into your life. You won't look back, except to see if someone is trying to steal Peri-Peri from the bush in your garden.

acknowledgements

A hot, heartfelt thank you to the following
individuals and organisations, in no particular order,
whose invaluable input helped to make this book possible.

Thank you to Robert Brozin, for keeping the dream alive – and for nursing the flame at times when some of us were battling to see its light.

Dr Bill Gallagher for access to his vast network of chefs and for his incredible support, fatherly wisdom and sober advice.

For helping us get around Mozambique and putting us in touch with the right people, we'd like to thank the ever-reliable Micki Perepeczko for being peri, peri helpful.

Charles, the agronomist, and Chico deserve thanks for their translation skills.

Johan, Piet, Mervyn and Jimmy of Farmers for God showed us around their farm and were incredibly hospitable and helpful.

Brendan and Jenny Evans, your Peri-Peri cheese is fantastic.

Breakfast and his family were kind enough to show us around their farm and pose for countless photographs in the hot sun, as was Arbeto.

We offer Fernando Huate, Peri-Peri sauce maker extraordinaire, our respect and thanks, and we are grateful to Lynne Joshua for putting us in touch with him and putting up with us.

Marianna Smith and Merle Dietrich, her Riches through Agriculture partner, were kind enough to let us spend time at Soetwaters, in the company of Cynthia Booys, Matilda Booys and Rina Goliath.

Dave de Wit and Mary Jane Wheeler for their dedication to the chilli cause and sharing so freely of their knowledge.

John Morris, Alison Parenzee and Michelle Wiener were unfailingly patient in teaching us about the science behind Peri-Peri.

Paul Ford, for sharing his incredible knowledge and passion for analytical aromachemistry.

The chefs from all over the world who shared with us their inventive and delicious Peri-Peri recipes.

Natalie Bell gets a special mention for her incredible talents as a stylist and for being a star generally. Thanks to (deep breath) Antiques By Hannes, Fabella, Garden Blue, Home Etc, Indaba, Inspired Solitude, Janet at Paraphenalia, Jonathan at Arthur Bales, La Busse Cour, Liebermann Potteries, Lulu at Lucky Fish, Objekt, Need, Die Ossewa, Pellerade and Studio Blue. These people and shops were all kind enough to help us with props and fabrics and all kinds of other interesting things.

The Cross Colours team for making the book so beautiful. Canda from Mattblack kindly facilitated our working relationship with the eminent Mike Saal. Thank you to Fred Swart for allowing us to use an idea of his for an illustration.

Bridget, Janet and Jenny from Jacana Media; Lineke from Imargo and the team at Gwynne Conlyn publishing..

And finally, Emma Redelinghuys managed to provide us with a pomegranate out of season, which was no mean feat.

bibliography

Alexander, Scott, *Introduction*, The Red Hot Jazz Archive: *A History of Jazz before 1930*, viewed 1 June 2007, http://www.redhotjazz.com/

Andrews, Jean, Peppers: *The Domesticated Capsicums* (Austin: University of Texas Press, 1995)

Asher, Gerald, Vineyard Tales: Reflections on Wine (San Francisco: Chronicle Books, 1996)

Barkham, Patrick, The Guardian, *Thai chillies that will have you dialling 999*, 4 October 2007, viewed 4 October 2007, http://www.guardian.co.uk/g2/story/0,,2183029,00.html

BBC News World Edition, *Chilli pepper link to arthritis pain*, 25 September 2002, viewed 11 June 2007, http://news.bbc.co.uk/2/hi/health/2281222.stm

Bosland, Paul W, *Capsicums: Innovative Uses of an Ancient Crop*, viewed 21 May 2007, http://www.hort.purdue.edu/newcrop/proceedings1996/V3-479.html

Collingham, Elizabeth M, Collingham, Lizzie, *Curry: A Tale of Cooks and Conquerors* (New York: Oxford University Press USA, 2006)

DeWitt, Dave, Pepper Profile: *African Birdseye*, viewed 6 July 2007, http://www.fiery-foods.com/dave/profile_birdseye.html

DeWitt, Dave and Bosland, Paul W, *Peppers of the World: An Identification Guide,* (Berkeley: Ten Speed Press, 1996)

DeWitt, Dave and Bosland, Paul W, *The Pepper Garden: An Identification Guide,* (Berkeley: Ten Speed Press, 1993)

DeWitt, Dave and Gerlach, Nancy, *The Whole Chile Pepper Book* (Boston: Little, Brown, 1990)

French, Jackie, *Book of Chilli* (Sydney: Angus & Robertson, 1994)
Goedverwacht, viewed 5 July 2007, http://www.places.co.za/html/goedverwacht.html

Goedverwacht: Steeped in History, viewed 5 July 2007,
http://www.tiscover.co.za/za/guide/5za,en,SCH1/objectId,RGN72za,curr,ZAR,season,at2,selectedEntry,home/home.html

Govindarajan, V.S. *Capsicum-Production, Technology, Chemistry and Quality, Part IV,* CRC Critical Reviews in Food Science and Nutrition, 1987, 25-3:185-282.

Hazen-Hammond, Susan and Fuss, Eduardo, *Chile Pepper Fever: Mine's Hotter Than Yours* (New Jersey: Gramercy Books, 1993)

Island of Mozambique, UNESCO World Heritage Centre, Updated 26 Sep 2007, viewed 27 September 2007, http://whc.unesco.org/en/list/599/

Krishna De, Amit (Ed.), *Capsicum: The Genus Capsicum* (Calcutta: CRC Press, 2003)

Maphosa, Tendai, *Drought Hits Zimbabwe Wheat Production*, 9 May 2005, viewed 27 June 2007, http://www.voanews.com/english/archive/2005-05/2005-05-09-voa17.cfm?CFID=153197934&CFTOKEN=63438479

Margen, Sheldon, *The Wellness Encyclopedia of Food and Nutrition: how to buy, store, and prepare every variety of fresh food.* (New York: Random House, 1992)

Nabhan, Gary Paul, *Why Some Like it Hot: Food, Genes and Cultural Diversity* (Washington, DC: Island Press, 2004)

Pearson, Michael, *The Indian Ocean* (London: Routledge, 2003)

Quelimane, viewed 29 June 2007, http://www.go2africa.com/Mozambique/beira/quelimane/

Robinson, Simon, *Global Warming*, Time, Vol. 169, No. 26, June 25 - July 2 2007, pp 77-80

Saccoccio, Sabrina, CBC News, *Who's umami? Human taste now comes in five flavours*, viewed 18 June 2007, http://www.cbc.ca/news/background/senses/umami.html

Turin, Luca, *The Secret of Scent: Adventures in Perfume and the Science of Smell*, (London: Faber & Faber, 2006)

Turner, Jack, *Spice: A History of Temptation* (London: HarperCollins, 2004)

Waldman, Amy, New York Times, *Four Tiny Isles off Mozambique*, 18 December 1994, viewed 27 September 2007, http://query.nytimes.com/gst/fullpage.html?res=9803E0D81F39F93BA25751C1A962958260.

http://www.peri-peri.com

index

recipe index

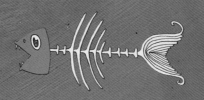